PENELOPE'S ROUTE

Karen Considine

Matador
9 Priory Business Park,
Wistow Road, Kibworth Beauchamp,
Leicestershire. LE8 0RX
Tel: 0116 279 2299
Email: books@troubador.co.uk
Web: www.troubador.co.uk/matador
Twitter: @matadorbooks

ISBN 978 1800460 690

British Library Cataloguing in Publication Data.
A catalogue record for this book is available from the British Library.

Printed and bound by CPI Group (UK) Ltd, Croydon, CR0 4YY

Matador is an imprint of Troubador Publishing Ltd

For my father, Pat Considine 1903-1975,
who understood my lust for adventure and
never wasted a "Be Careful" on me.

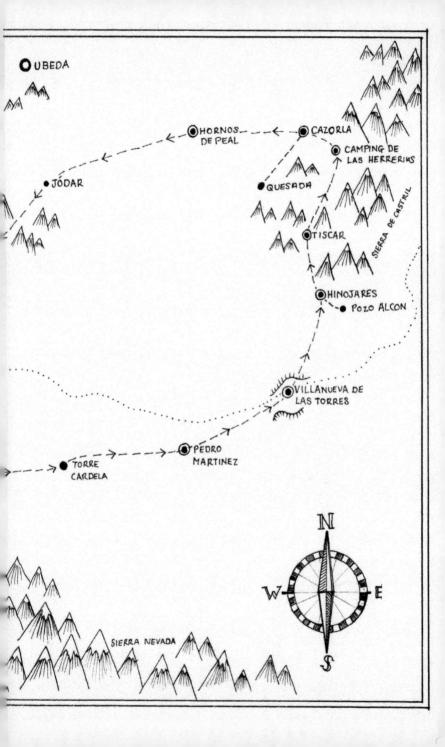

"I would sooner be a foreigner in Spain than in most countries. How easy it is to make friends in Spain!"

— George Orwell

*

April 1st

Fools' Weather

April Fools' Day, and the first rain in four months chose to fall in torrents on Southern Andalusia. I stood on the side of the road, carless and drenched. The trailer containing my two equine companions on this adventure, Luqa and Bruma, should swish by any moment and pick me up. Dan, the buckaroo from Oregon whose act of purchasing my horse-trekking business had left me free to set this plan in motion, was driving us and I had left my car at a friend's house, full of horse feed which would be needed on my travels later in the month. My phone vibrated under several layers of mackintosh and I read the WhatsApp through the drips off my hat. It was from Dan, and, ominously, at least three times as long as his usual succinct missives.

"Truck broke down just past Jimena. Won't make it today. Shall I unload horses and ride them back or tie them up at roadside bar?"

What? Thus can much-prepared plans and long-awaited projects be scuppered in half an hour.

"Do NOT unload horses. I'll think of something…"

Sotogrande is smart so the Soto supermarket has a shelter for its trolleys. As the rain thrummed on the roof, I balanced on one, calling everyone I could think of with a tow bar. Tito, reliable, funny, Argentine polo friend came up trumps. He was there in twenty damp minutes; we drove the fifteen kilometres back to Jimena, pushed Dan´s dead pickup out from under the trailer bar, hitched up Tito´s truck and set off for Granada. I was in such a state of expectancy and panic, I scarcely gave a thought to Dan´s poor wife, Shannon, sitting by the side of the road in the broken vehicle waiting for a tow truck or to Tito, our saviour, who handed the keys of his pick-up to Dan and jumped out in the downpour on the side of the road as we repassed Sotogrande, racing home for the birth of his granddaughter.

In the back seat of the truck we had stuffed my saddle and bridle and sheepskin plus anything we could squeeze in, taken in from the downpour out of the pack saddle that contained everything I thought I would need for a month riding across Granada and Jaen provinces. Most importantly, I had rescued my guide and companion, Penelope Chetwode´s book 'Two Middle-Aged Ladies in Andalusia', from imminent drowning in the unprotected flatbed where all the remaining and less delicate stuff was trying to hide from the lashing rain under an inadequate tarpaulin.

Penelope and I had a long way to go and I needed her by my side.

In 1961, Penelope Valentine Chetwode Betjeman came to Spain to see friends and join in a ride with them across part of Malaga Province. Having completed what she described as *"this enchanting conducted tour across the Serrania de Ronda"*, she decided she would like to see more of a then virtually untouched part of Spain. Borrowing a horse from her friend the Duke of Wellington, she set off on a circular and very loosely planned route. This took her northeast from Granada across rolling plains, north through the mountains of Cazorla to Ubeda and then south west via the Magina mountain range eventually returning to where she started from.

My mother gave me her book when I was fifteen and I was fascinated. Firstly, of course, by the magical adventure of riding off into the unknown but also by how the people she met on her journey lived, and where they lived. It was all so very different from my childhood in country Ireland. So that was how the idea for this jaunt I was on in 2019 had begun. Fifty- eight years after Penelope set off on her borrowed mare, La Marquesa, I was planning on following in her hoof prints across the high, dry, stretching landscape of southern Spain.

After four and a half hours of peering through mad-ly-slashing windscreen wipers, we arrived in the village of Illora, north of the city of Granada, and then drove into Molino del Rey. This is the Duke of Wellington´s estate, given to the first "Iron" Duke and his descendants by Fernando Vll, King of Spain, for services rendered during the Napoleonic occupation. (These services are described by Penelope as *"driving Napoleon out of Spain"* and my lack of historical knowledge means I can neither confirm nor deny whether he did it single handed...) On the way up the long drive an impressive aqueduct runs alongside, once vital for the land and the olive-pressing in the "Molino del Rey" – the Mill of the King. Jute used to be grown on the estate especially for the mats through which they pressed the olives to extract the oil, but now the mill is silent.

We were expected up at the yard behind the main house and Don Javier, "apoderado" or manager of the estate, was waiting for us. With him were quite a few random Josés and Antonios who unadvisedly waved our truck and trailer into the inner sanctum of the stables where it was immediately quite obvious there was no way Dan was going to be able to turn the rig.

When Penelope came here to choose her horse she was shown around by an Irish equivalent of Don Javier, Eudo Thonson-Rye, who firmly led her away from the elegant Andalusian and Hispano-Arab horses in the main stables by the house and down to the mule stud at the mill. Mule "trains" were still the easiest and most efficient way of moving cargo across this countryside sixty years ago. The present Duke told me how there were at least thirty brood mares at the stud and he particularly remembered a donkey stallion called Leon. Mules are the produce of a mare and a donkey and cannot reproduce so Leon would have been called upon year after year to impregnate all those different ladies, surely a boy donkey's dream. For Penelope, Eudo led out a mare called La Marquesa. With a practical figure and a Roman nose, she was not the dashing steed Penelope had secretly hoped for but, as the agent pointed out, she was a "good doer", accustomed to any local fodder she might be offered and was available because she had not come in (mule) foal that year. When Penelope ascertained that the Marquesa was twelve, roughly equivalent in horse years to her own fifty-one, she thought with satisfaction that they were two middle-aged ladies setting off to explore Andalusia together.

*

Because Penelope's journey had started and finished at Molino del Rey, I had been keen to see if my horses could also overnight here so we would set out from the same place. The present Duke of Wellington voiced an interest in meeting me and was due to be in Spain in March when I was visiting my newly married brother in Canada. There was just one morning, before he caught a plane from Granada, when it looked as if we might be able to get together. So I got off the plane from Vancouver at Malaga airport, still wearing clothes for snow, went straight home and picked up the dog, bought several cans of Red Bull, got in my car and set off on the long drive to Illora through the dawn. His Grace met me in the archives and administration building which used to be the little sham Gothic estate chapel where Penelope went to mass before her departure. I was delighted to hear that, as a boy, the duke had loved riding the Marquesa in the school holidays. He knew her well so it was rather nice to meet someone who had such a close link with one of the two middle-aged ladies. He also reminisced about his grandfather, Penelope's friend, known as Gerry, who liked to tour the estate by mule cart. The mule man, who was in charge of preparing the turnout with two mules in hand, was expected to wear livery when he was driving the carriage. I had visions of poor Curro or Paco gently melting in full livery on a hot Spanish summer's day while His Grace inspected his rolling acres. The archives held several copies of Penelope's book and it was grand to be able to see a first edition with far more photos than the later publications. With permission I snapped away like mad with my phone so I had something to show the villages I would ride through.

It was still only ten in the morning when I left my meeting

at Molino del Rey and shaping up to be a very hot day. My car was overheating so, after a lifetime of old bangers, I knew to turn on the heat inside the car full blast to get the hot air out of the engine. What with that, temperatures in the high 20º's and an excess of Red Bull masking massive jet lag, I drove home in a euphoric state, quite sure that the Duke's obvious interest and encouragement gave me the green light for ploughing ahead with my PLAN! He was the first person I had met who did not think that I was at least slightly batty to consider celebrating my sixty-seventh birthday on the back of a horse in unknown country one week into a month-long ride.

*

On this, the first day of April and of my adventure, everything looked rather different. The lashing rain had slowed to a drizzle and it was just cold and damp and grey. We unloaded the horses into two of the stables which had been cleared of an awful lot of "stuff" since I was last here and filled with deep golden straw. Dan helped me stack under cover what looked like a ridiculous amount of gear. Then he and many willing helpers, all of whom were trying to hide the fact that they were dying to dance jigs and reels (or Sevillanas and Pasodobles) to celebrate the long, long awaited rain on their poor, parched land, unhitched the trailer and spun it round. Dan did a sixteen point turn in the pickup, re-hitched and he was off on the long drive back to the Serrania de Ronda.

So… here I was, or should I say we were. The heads of Bruma, small round dun mare from the hills of Ronda and named after the "misty" morning when I bought her, and

Luqa, Hispano-Arab gelding, (Shaluqa means Levante wind in Arabic), peered over His Grace's stable doors wondering if supper was a possibility or if they should just go on eating the rather delicious straw. It must have been wonderful when these stables were fully occupied by fine Spanish horses, but now, rather surreally, they seemed to be fully occupied by canaries. Among my reception committee was the estate security guard, Ramon, and his wife, Emilia, who asked me into their house on the stable yard for tea and sticky cakes. The canaries turned out to be hers – hundreds of them in and out of cages of all shapes and sizes. There were beige and white and yellow and golden and fiery-red canaries. Those that were not singing and chatting and pecking and tweeting and fluttering were laying eggs and sitting on them. Indeed a lot of them were sitting on eggs so there will doubtless be another hundred canaries in whatever the gestation time of a canary egg is; my guess is not long. My horse dealer's mind immediately presumed this was a cash crop but Emilia smiled contentedly and assured me it was just her hobby.

She and Ramon, both in their fifties and somewhat portly, are local, and she told me how happy they have been working here for twenty years. Like everyone else I met on the estate, they talked as if they were all one family. They take pride in the way it is run and the present Duke's dedication to conserving the agriculture and traditional ways of doing things which are being lost to a great extent in the wider province of Granada. There are old olives whose trunks are works of art, replanted and saved from extinction near Illora village where they were to be sacrificed for younger better-fruiting trees. Down by the elegant aqueduct the mill is being renovated too. Don Javier, who is tall and dark, very charming and I would think a very good "agent" for the estate, told me they are using all wooden rafters, no steel or concrete. Emilia's daughter Isabel was told to stop doing her homework while I was there and pay attention to what I was telling them about my planned ride! She is in her teens and studying hard and her older sister is working in a smart hotel. In Penelope's time there would have been no question of the girls aspiring to jobs - there was not even enough work to go round for the sons of the large families that were the norm then.

Ramon drove me into Illora to the hostel where I was staying and Paqui, my landlady, was so intrigued with my story and my plans I really thought she might never leave my bedroom. She got hugely excited and asked question after question as I sat surrounded by a motley collection of bags that were really more than I could carry and yet still lacked things I needed for the night. Pack-saddle organising was new to me and I did feel slightly ashamed that Penelope managed without a pack horse, but her needs were somewhat different to mine.

In 1961 the countryside I was now planning to ride across was seething with working animals, mainly mules and donkeys but horses were used as transport and for ploughing. The mules were cargo carriers – grain and olives from the land to the mills, flour and oil to the cities and to the railways, and "cantaros", the large terracotta water carriers, from pottery to market. In the villages everyone had a donkey carrying these vessels with which they fetched water from the central springs and pumps and fountains to their houses on a daily basis. The Spanish do not say it is "raining cats and dogs", they say it is raining "a cantaros". The proliferation and necessity of working animals meant that there were farriers and leather workers in each small town so the traveller on a horse could get his beast re-shod, his equipment fixed, and find animal feed at every stop. Not so in 2019, therefore I was carrying extra horse shoes, tools and nails, spare reins, stirrup leathers and cinch, and emergency oats, just in case. Nor was I relying on finding people along my paths to ask the way – shepherds and goatherds are disappearing out here since the monoculture of olives started to take over, so I had paper maps, Google Earth and Wikiloc to help me out. This means that dreaded word of our era -"devices"- plus spare battery packs for the nights with no mains electricity.

In Bruma's pack I also carried a translation for each village of what Penelope had written about them. This took me hours and hours at home in the weeks leading up to my departure, but I wanted to have something to offer the people along the way. To be honest, I needed a reason to explain my sudden eccentric appearance in their midst, in the hopes they would help me on my mission, which I was calling "La Ruta de Penelope"

Penelope would not have had to lug her luggage any great distance from her horse in 1961: there was at least one "posada", or lodging place for people and their animals, in the centre of every village. All the traveller had to do was ride their horse or donkey, or drive their sheep or mule train or pigs into the village and ask the first person they met where the "posada" was. There they had everything laid on in the way of food for themselves and their animals, a bedroom and stabling downstairs, often partly below ground level, for the livestock. Of course the primitive conditions left a lot to be desired and Penelope is delightfully honest about some of the drawbacks.

"To sum up, posada life must be entered into in a spirit of adventure. The lack of modern comforts and gastronomic pleasures....will soon be forgiven and forgotten if you decide to become a posada specialist: to enjoy, in each new inn you come to, the different distortions to which the mirror subjects your face, the angle at which the washstand leans over to left or right, the beauty of the pumpkins and pomegranates and pimientos drying in the spare bedroom, and the skill required to fill your hot water bottle with a ladle from a frying pan - for the kettle is unknown in Southern Spain."

The kettle is still unknown in Andalusia but I had brought my secret weapon, a tiny camping gas stove, which was to stand me in good stead for hot soups and hot water bottles throughout the vagaries of the weather in store for me. However, as I burrowed into my extraordinarily squeaky bed on the very first night following in Penelope's footsteps, I had no idea what lay ahead and just felt glad I had a loo next door and would not have to make nightly forays down to the stables as Penelope did.

"The technique of using stable sanitation successfully and without undue strain on the nerves is as follows: when you want to enter the stable to attend to your horse, you open the door with a smile on your face, switch on the light and advance towards the animal, welcoming any help from your landlord or fellow-guest which may be offered. When, however, you wish to enter for the other purpose you go towards the door with a look of grim determination upon your face, do not turn on the light, and slam the door hard behind you. Should you hear a giant pee-ing close by it is almost certain to be a mule or a donkey: and when your eyes, growing used to the dim light, discern the figure of your landlady squatting in a corner, the custom is for both of you to roar with laughter as if this

clandestine meeting is the most natural thing in the world, which indeed it is."

Good on you Penelope Chetwode - you are going to be a hard woman to follow.

*

April 2nd

Lost in the olives, late in the square

If that bed was not doing service in the original "posada" of Illora, it definitely had forbears there. The springs grabbed me by each individual vertebra and then complained bitterly if I shifted so much as an inch. This, combined with high excitement, made for a practically sleepless night so I rose from my screaming bed in the cold pre-dawn dark, dressed and crept down the steep stairs, clutching my myriad plastic bags and rucksack. Leaving the keys on the hall table and slamming the door behind me, I peered across at the bar that everyone, but everyone, had told me opened at 6am to give coffee and "tostadas" to the workers of Illora. Pitch black street, everything firmly closed, cold wind and nearly an hour until Ramon was due to pick me up.

I had lectured myself on remembering to eat well on this trip, and a good breakfast was part of the plan. Not a great start. I spotted a lit doorway at the top of the chilly street and transferred everything including myself into a bank entrance porch that sheltered the cash point. At least I was out of the wind. After a little while, a series of very well turned-out local businessmen and women started coming in and out which was a little surprising and must speak of the prosperity of this village, surrounded by olive groves producing their indispensable oil and close enough to Granada city to be on the tourist route. Some of the visitors to my porch were at the screen for quite a while sorting out their personal accounts, I presume. All were slightly taken aback by the horse hair covered bag lady and her chattels sheltering in the corner. Out of the doorway I could see the Moorish castle floodlit high above us and the 16th century church where the Duke of Wellington´s daughter, Lady Charlotte, was married. I thought longingly of the bacon and eggs that Penelope had for breakfast at Molino del Rey before she set out on the first day of her trek.

As the sky lightened, Ramon turned up in his jeep to fetch me. The horses were delighted and a little relieved to see me and get their equivalent of a fry-up for breakfast, a delicious high speed, high sports oat mixture, and plenty of it!

Emilia´s "hobby" was shouting in two hundred canary voices and I said to Ramon,

"Listen to those birds"

"Yes" he said "In Spring they think they are free in the woods".

Sad.

So the moment had finally come to prepare and load my two horses for real. I had lain in that vociferous bed and gone through it all over and over but I still set about it with trepidation. My pack saddle is my pride and joy. It was in the indispensable bible for all long distance riders, The Horse Travel Handbook, that I read about a man, Kelly Destrake, who makes the packs everyone recommends. His company is in the north of British Colombia and, as I was going to Vancouver Island in March to meet my brother's new wife, it seemed it was meant to be. I ordered a saddle and had it shipped to Bill's house and brought it back to Spain with me. Before I found out about the Custom Pack Rigging Co., I had spent hours trying to memorise knots with names like latigo, box hitch, diamond hitch, cowboy night latch, which were apparently essential for roping a pack saddle onto a horse or mule. My Canadian pack needs no ropes at all; it has a base that adjusts to any pack animal's back with metal crossbars to hook two big canvas paniers on. The secret is to balance them well so you haven't got a lopsided horse, to which end I had bought myself a hand scales and throughout my journey I weighed each bag as I loaded it on one side or the other.

Penelope's packing list, noted in detail in her book, embarrassed me somewhat in its minimalism but in the end I needed pretty well everything I took.

PENELOPE: Quite a selection of books including Richard Ford's 'Gatherings from Spain' written in 1846, 'Don Quixote', a dictionary, the Spanish Catechism and St Peter of Alcantara for Spanish-reading practice

KAREN: What turned out to be a really awful novel on my Kindle, 'The Long Riders'Guild Horse Travel Handbook', 'Spanish Raggle Taggle' by Starkie and 'Two Middle-Aged Ladies in Andalusia' by Penelope Chetwode

P: 2 Exercise books for diary and notes

K: Ditto

P: Sponge Bag

K: Ditto except mine probably had a lot more emergency medicines than hers. We fuss more now, don't we?

P: Hot water bottle

K: Ditto – thank goodness. It was a last minute addition.

After that I have to confess Penelope´s packing and mine hardly coincided at all as she was including such things as a Terylene skirt rolled in an old stocking, two pairs of nylons, a mauve jersey, and 4 handkerchiefs. Also such indispensable items, in 1961, as shoe polish, mending things, face powder and film for her camera.

We coincided in our dress somewhat, both wearing broad brimmed sombreros and tying coats (hers tweed) and waterproofs on the saddle. Though I have to confess she was turned out better than me with a collar and tie! We also both hung a leather "bota", the Spanish version of a flask, off our saddle. Hers only carried lemonade, mine was filled to the top with whiskey. Penelope professed to loathing spirits and seemed to avoid alcohol generally, which is the one thing about her I might have found unnerving.

My pack saddle contained, in separate bags and bundles:

- horse first aid kit
- horseshoes and shoeing kit
- my gas stove and emergency food rations
- sleeping bag
- small rucksack with my clothes
- spare tack
- 2nd pair of shoes for me
- Ipad, cables and battery packs
- Oats for the horses as necessary
- Folding buckets
- Bag with letters to Town Halls, translations, my journal, books, maps etc.

After over an hour and a lot of peering at Bruma from every angle, I decided she was evenly loaded. Luqa was waiting, saddled up, and the inevitable moment had come – we were off!

With my little group of Molino del Rey friends waving farewell, we rode into the morning mist, crossing the beautiful pasturelands, half seen against the rising sun. Beside the little lake on the estate, ducks rose from the water and the horses pricked their ears and jogged. We were feeling good. We entered the olive groves, intending, as Penelope had, to cut diagonally past Illora and emerge to cross the main road beyond. One of the advantages of olives is they don't escape or wander onto the road and get run over so there is virtually no fencing anywhere, unlike the livestock-filled mountains of Ronda where I live. After yesterday's rain it was muddy underfoot and the mud in these parts is slippery clay and deep, so I said a little prayer about the horses keeping their shoes on. A local man collecting wild asparagus was astonished to see me with my two horses, confirmation that equines are very rare here now. I proudly told him that this was the first day of my adventure which would take me as far as Cazorla and back. Feeling that I was surely on the very route taken by Penelope, I trotted across the undulating groves for about an hour until we came across a "barranco". These, I was to learn, criss-cross the hills and are deep stream beds with sheer sides and no passing places. Why should there be if the olive groves belong to different people? No foot traffic, no mules; this is my side, that is yours; why should we need to traverse this great divide?

We waded uphill through the slippery mud and found no

access over the quarry-like gully below us and then slithered back the other way, still looking, until I thought we were lost. But no – there was my friend still picking asparagus. The "barranco" had led us full circle. I was mortified! He grinned broadly but did not comment and I pulled my hat down over my eyes and slunk past.

So we went back and slap through the middle of town, then along the ferocious main road with so many lorries passing that Luqa, who thinks he is frightened of them, in the end just shut his eyes and stopped until they had passed.

I was now in the wrong place to take Penelope's route and anyway she had had trouble with a steep descent into Moclín, so we found a lovely contoured path via Puerto Lope. By this time we were much later than planned and I had unadvisedly told Manuel Caba, historian of Moclín, that we would be there well before lunchtime. This was a valuable lesson I learned on that first day - never give anyone an ETA when you are on a long ride. Things happen. If you are in good time they look at you in slight irritation and say "But you're early" and, if you are late, "We were worried", accusingly. You can tell them when you hope to leave but NEVER when you hope to arrive! An hour before we had even begun the climb to Moclín, Manuel was phoning me all of a dither. He had a reception committee waiting in the village square which included the Mayoress and the Guardia Civil. It was no good, I told him, it would take as long as it took. He was cross with us. Obviously not a horseman, he suggested I "put my foot down".

We rode into Moclín in hot sun as the clock struck two and down into the square at five past. Not a sign of anyone.

The welcoming party had lost interest and drifted off. Tying up to convenient trees, I belted into the Town Hall as the doors were closing and left the letter from the Mayor of Gaucin and my translation of Penelope Chetwode's pages about Moclín with a lady who said she would give them to the Mayoress. She then informed me that my horses could not stay in the square – what if they ate the flowers? I felt this was a bit much after my enormous efforts with the translation but, admittedly, as we emerged the horses were gorging on mustard yellow and blood red daisies from the flower beds and, worse still, had both lifted their tails and deposited huge piles of dung on the pristine fancy stonework. Andalusian villages now pride themselves on spotless streets, everything paved, flowers in urns and pots at every opportunity, not at all horse friendly as were the dirt lanes and sandy streets of another era. I trudged up the hill with them to a large grassy area under the castle, once a threshing floor, and tied them in the shade.

Up above the streets of the village to the west, I could see the scary descent that Penelope and La Marquesa had accomplished. At one point, deciding she had better dismount on the uphill side, Penelope slid right under her mare's belly and was mistakenly trodden on.

Moclín is a very beautiful hilltop village, one of the seven villages of the "Vega" (or plain) of Granada, though far from being on the plain itself. Dominated by a huge Moorish Castle, it gazes south from the top of its little mountain to the glistening snowy peaks of the Sierra Nevada and north and east to countless hilltops stretching away below. Many of these are crowned with "alcalas" or watchtowers. In this castle the Spanish Catholic king and queen waited for six years, planning and negotiating, before riding forth to take Granada and his beloved Alhambra from the last of the Moorish monarchs,

I found Manuel Caba, a slight man in his seventies, immaculately turned out and, somewhat mollified by my apologies for our late arrival, he took me to the house where Penelope and La Marquesa had spent their first night. There was no "posada" even then in Moclin, but one of the old boys, whom she had asked as he stood gossiping with his mates by the water trough, took her down the cobbled street to a little house and spoke to a young woman who turned out to be his daughter-in-law, Eugenia.

"She angelically agreed to put up the Marquesa and myself for the night. We had some difficulty persuading the old girl to go in through the front door which was rather low and she was rather tall. I pulled and coaxed while the old man pushed and shouted. Together we got her safely into the living room of the little house: the floor was paved with stone but a path of cobbles led across it from the front door to the stable door at the back...Meanwhile Eugenia's husband Fernando had appeared, a gentle young man of twenty-seven with a saintly smile."

Eugenia had an eight-month old baby daughter, Maria, who was spoon fed on cereal and goats' milk while her mother and the strange foreign woman, had a cosy chat about the merits of breast feeding. As at this, the beginning of her journey, Penelope maintains she had no Spanish at all except a few set phrases about who she was and where she came from, I would have loved to have been a fly on the wall for that conversation. Later a supper of broth, an omelette and fresh sardines was prepared by the young mother who had cooked for the gentry in Malaga before her marriage and therefore had something of a repertoire in the kitchen. Fernando was very deaf and the rosary, said nightly in most Spanish households of that time, included prayers for his recovery.

Penelope was a converted Catholic and therefore more devout than most of us born into the Faith with an occasional token nod in the direction of the bells and the smells. She notes all the prayers and masses, catechisms and intentions along the way in which she joined with huge enthusiasm, never missing a chance to attend Holy Mass. However she wasn't just waiting for God to do his bit in this case: though we learn of Fernando's deafness in the book we do not learn of her kindness. Manuel, who was about twelve at the time, remembers how she came back several times to the village after that first visit bringing and fitting a hearing aid for Fernando. She used to ride in from Molino del Rey quite frequently and became good friends with Eugenia and Fernando. I ask Manuel how he remembers her.

"Muy decidida y muy alegre" – "Very determined and very cheerful".

Now, the house where the young couple lived has a huge modern doorway you could fit an elephant through and the building has been renovated and re-renovated several times. How could Fernando, his legs wrapped in calico, cheap sandals on his feet as he set out for work paid by the day, afford an enormous house like this? Manuel thinks that the old gentleman, Fernando's father, who first led Penelope to the house and lived with them, left a good inheritance when he died which enabled the young couple to improve things. From a higher street at the back you can look down into the yard where La Marquesa spent the night with pigs and chickens.

Alas, Fernando died young, struck by a motorbike as he waited at a traffic-light on his bicycle. He must have been a long way from home – I hadn't seen any traffic-lights anywhere yet, and I wondered just a little at the efficacy of the hearing aid. Baby Maria married a man from Ibiza and took her mother with her so, although Eugenia still comes back to visit, I was not going to meet her this time. I would love to have met someone who was so friendly with Penelope.

Manuel used to drive all over Granada Province delivering animal feed and veterinary supplies and he remembers Eudo Tonsen-Rye's wife, Rosemary, at Molino del Rey always ordering "rat food", by which she meant poison. Water mills were a popular haven for rodents. We sat down in the shade of a restaurant by the square and he seemed intrigued by the goings-on at the Duke of Wellington's Spanish estate. In spite of his dedication to the accuracy of local Moclín history, he was not above a bit of scandalous gossip and certainly seemed to know more about the British Royal Family than I do. I kept steering him back to the matter in hand but, while questioning incorrect historical accounts pertaining to things he knows the truth of, he had no qualms about believing the most scurrilous contemporary press reports!

He is a perfect example of the changes wrought in these villages in two generations. His father and grandfather farmed the land. He lives in the same "finca" or farm but has not dedicated all his life to it. When he retired from his delivery job he started sculpting iron. He presented me with one of his pieces, thin wrought iron, casually curved, a few lines and yet so obviously a cat sunning itself. Later I looked up his blog. It is impressive. All his children are architects and doctors, married to teachers and other doctors. They all live in Granada. However proud the new generations of parents are of their children, it means that the villages are emptying of family. Moclín is now filling up with a random collection of foreigners, stunned by the beauty of this stalwart castle on its rock and the lacy vision of the Sierra Nevada floating above the plain below. Penelope was the first, the very first, of these benign foreign invaders and that is why she is remembered.

Lunch was something of an international affair in the bar in the square starting with two English friends, Ian and Andrew, who live in the village and are renovating a gorgeous house from which – on a clear day and with the binoculars - they can see the Alhambra. There was also a Frenchman, Frederic who is uncovering the old trails in the mountains and is married to a relative of Manuel´s. A woman from Belgium then joined us. She was walking to Santiago for the next three months which certainly put my little venture in the shade and, of course, Manuel, now thawed from his fury with me and toasting my enterprise in sweet and sparkling Cava.

The Cava, and eating an enormous lunch to make up for lack of breakfast, turned out to be a mistake on my part as the afternoon became hotter and hotter. With moral support from Ian and Andrew, I decided to swap the pack onto Luqa. He had not yet figured out that setting off every day as if he was in a tearing hurry, pulling and jogging and dancing was both unnecessary and unwise. He was weary from our twenty plus kilometres so far and, as soon as I made him the pack pony, he changed persona and became a relaxed, steady beast of burden, his nose never passing in front of my knee as I rode Bruma along.

We set off down the steep "Camino del Gollizno", the same path Penelope took but now, unfortunately, cemented in parts. As this is very narrow and definitely a path for mountain bikers, walkers and horsemen only, I could not see how the slippery and heat-reflecting concrete helped anyone. I dismounted and led when it became dangerously smooth and precipitous and heard footsteps running to catch up with us. A handsome, lanky Frenchman drew level with a huge smile and then his face fell.

"I thought you were someone else."

Really? On a tiny path in the middle of the crags and gorges with not a house in sight?

"Yes, I have a friend, a girl, who is taking two horses around Spain. She just leads them, never rides."

Then he turned sadly and walked his weary way back up to the little chapel on the mountain where he planned on spending the night.

Jaysus, we're all at it, and some are barmier than me!

As the path levelled out a bit I remounted a reluctant Bruma who was obviously considering going to live in France where people didn't actually get on their horse.

Penelope's route, which she took the morning after her night in Moclín, led us through a village called Olivares, deep in the river valley and then climbed gently, skirting along the lower slopes of a small range of craggy hills. We, however, were riding it all in the evening and reached the village of Colomera as darkness fell. Here I had made a friend called José Eduardo who had a small equestrian centre with room for the horses. The "Posada" where I stayed used to belong to his grandparents and he runs it as a small hotel. There are no animals any more but looking down from my bedroom at the flower-filled patio which used to be the stables I could swear I saw a load of tortoises waddling about. Of course it might have been due to weariness and whiskey...

Clockwise from top left: Leaving Molino Del Rey. Manolo, historian of Moclin. Jose Eduardo, in the sombrero, and his riders

＊

April 3rd

Bold bad Bruma

Back in November, when "la ruta de Penelope" was just an idea, I decided I had better come and inspect the lands across which I was considering riding alone for a month. I chose a few days that looked as if they would be fine but my car then developed an embarrassing incontinence problem which had to be fixed before I went anywhere. So in the end my Uruguayan friend, Marcela, and I set off in bleak winter rain. As the sleet slashed down, the wind whined across the flat land and the olive trees sat sullenly with their feet in the water, we drove around the villages Penelope visited during the first week of her trip and looked at each other in horror.

"No shade if it's hot."

"No shelter if it's wet."

"Where are the animals?"

"Where are the people?"

Even Marcela, the best of friends and a true optimist, born one of nine children in an estancia on the rolling open spaces of South America, found our surroundings forbidding.

Having booked into the 'Posada de Colomera', we turned

up for the night and owner, José Eduardo Escudero, met us at the door with his riding boots on! By the time we were through the door into the shelter of the hall I had told him my plan, and before we even had a room key he was telling us about all the horse trails he had mapped in the area and how to draw your own trail in advance on Wikiloc!

He had come back to his family's village in early middle age, leaving a well paid job in Madrid because he got fed up "with the corruption and the stress". He is a tall, gentle, amiable man, usually in his boots about to go to or return from his small and successful equestrian centre. Together with his wife, Meli, and two children in their twenties he runs his grandparents' "posada" as a little hotel without, alas, the animals (unless you count hallucinatory tortoises). His businesses benefit, as do those in the village of Illora, from the proximity of the city of Granada. The fact that there were stables for my horses was a big plus.

After we had spent another day cruising the countryside in the driving rain and my dog had eaten every seatbelt in the car and Marcela's had had a bilious attack from the stress of it all, I had decided to go ahead with the PLAN.

*

José Eduardo had championed my scheme from the start, helping me talk to Town Halls and rediscover Penelope's routes in his area, so when, today, he said that he and some clients would like to accompany me part of the way on this, my second day's riding, I was delighted.

The clients turned out to be complete beginners but José

Eduardo plonked them on a couple of horses, showed them right and left and stop and sent them to the front to lead us. No helmets or introductory lessons or any of that rubbish, and they were soon hanging on and loving it. Straight away we headed down a steep hill covered in almond trees whose unripe fruit, shell and all, our guide offered to my horses. They crunched with alacrity and, for the rest of my trek, helped themselves off the trees whenever they got the chance. One of the beginners was riding a mare with a foal at foot that took a fancy to Luqa and kept investigating his undercarriage in case there was a milk supply. This affront to his manhood, combined with the tiny dolly steps he had to do not to overtake the meandering progress of the horses in front, would have challenged the patience of a lesser horse but he munched on the almonds and rose above it, literally. We passed a 2nd century Roman bridge over the stream in the valley and climbed again to a Moorish necropolis, hiding in hummocky grass and rocks high on the hill looking back to the castle of Colomera.

Penelope took a lower road than ours, now asphalt, following a little river in the valley. Here she met Francisco Martinez riding behind a boy on a large donkey, probably the original Andalusian breed which are enormous. Known as "El Asno Andaluz" they are believed to be the oldest of the European breeds with a three thousand year history and are now, sadly, in danger of extinction. Francisco invited this unexpected foreign woman to his house. They crossed the stream and rode along the far bank until they came to his part cave home, "Santo Domingo", where she spent a very sociable evening, visiting neighbours and even going out with her host and his gun looking for partridge among the poplars. She describes his leisurely life with two grown sons running the small holding and three daughters and his wife doing all the work of the household. He told her how the hill I was riding over nearly sixty years later, used to be infested with bandits, mainly those from the losing side of the Civil War, who were a great nuisance as they used to come down and demand half of everything from the valley dwellers. They were finally cleared out by government forces in the mid 1950's. John Betjeman, Penelope's husband, had been so worried about the lawless reputation of southern Spain that he had written to implore her to take out an insurance policy in the bank in Seville as he would not be able to pay a ransom for her. Penelope was able to reassure him, before she set out alone, that the situation had much improved over the previous decade and the land was now law-abiding.

It was here that she made her first attempt to drink out of a "porron", the long spouted glass wine container that you tip and drink from without it touching your mouth. The wine went all over her face! There was no electricity in the valley and they used home-produced olive oil in their lamps, which were rather smoky, and for the fire burnt straw chaff and olive prunings. I would love to have ridden along that little river to "Santo Domingo" to see what the descendants of Francisco Martinez were up to but the house he was so proud of and the little valley where they farmed are now under the still jewel-blue waters of a reservoir.

One of Franco's lasting and more positive legacies is the many reservoirs or "pantanos" he instigated all over Spain, which have bolstered the country's economy and agriculture. Extreme weather reports on Spanish television – drought or flood – always mention the level of the reservoirs. Colomera "pantano" was one of the later ones, started in 1982 and now irrigating the monotonous hills of olives. The little stream that spawned it could only have watered smallholdings of crops and vegetables, leaving some stretches of wild land, ideal for a bit of rough shooting.

Little did Francisco know, when he entertained Penelope, that in twenty years his children's legacy would be drowned.

By mid-morning not only my horses were champing at the bit to get a move on. With a long day's ride ahead, I was beginning to find the dawdling pace of our little group unbearable, so I was glad when our ways parted and they turned for home. We three intrepid travellers accelerated away into the undiscovered "campo", a much used word in all Hispanic countries for everywhere that is open and rural and potentially exciting.

I halted the horses in the village of Benalua de las Villas to drink deeply at the same cool shaded trough as La Marquesa. Then we passed what is now the Co-op where Penelope saw sugar beet being loaded onto a lorry and a fifty-foot long chaff rick. Tractors were revving up for some project in the olive groves and a trailer full of olive branches drove by.

Just before we stopped for lunch in some lush knee-deep grass, we passed a once magnificent manor farmhouse, or "cortijo", called "De Anda". It was crumbling now and the surrounding land was a little oasis of arable in a sea of olives but there was a pretty bridge over the stream to it and a grand entrance, and the poppies and cornflowers growing against the once white walls were every bit as good as an herbaceous border. Just outside a tall man stopped me, his face lighting up at the sight of the horses and even more intrigued with my pack saddle. He was so delightful and so courteous I actually dismounted and showed him how it worked, unhooking a panier and proudly demonstrating the hinges on the base that allow it to fit any animal´s back. It turned out he was Juan ("or Juanito because everyone around here has known me from knee high") owner of the vast, romantic, tumbling down "cortijo" beside us. He was sad as he told me about the only animal he has left who is an old mule. He loves her but feels he should sell her as he has no more use for her. I did my best to persuade him to keep her in the beautiful courtyard where she was born, with the daily feeds she is used to. He was a truly lovely man and if he could just win the lottery so we could rescue that amazing place I might even consider marrying him, throwing in the pack saddle as dowry. Of course if I hear he sold the mule, it is all off!

After lunch, leaving the little lanes behind, we turned north into the campo, the Sierra Nevada still visible on the horizon, yesterday´s mud drying out and the spicy scent of olive trees in the air. The sun shone out of a clear sky and, high on the beauty of it all, we headed gently uphill through the groves, turning to admire the views in every direction. Hoopoes hopped and "hoo-ed" all around us, sounding exactly like someone blowing into an empty bottle, and I unclipped Bruma from her lead, pretty sure she would not stray far from us in this strange land. She then worked on a system where she found a nice bit of grass and stayed to eat as much as she could until she lost sight of us, catching up at the gallop. Eventually we came to some little fields of wheat and barley and she reckoned this was all planted just for her. Fearing both for the precious crops and the pack when her catch-up dashes started to include high bucks, I tried to grab her again from Luqa´s back but she wasn´t having that. Eventually I had to get off him and stalk her till I caught her, she had got so above herself. Another half an hour and we were climbing a steep slope while I, with all leads and reins in my right hand, was drinking from my water bottle. Without warning, deprived of her grazing, the bold little baggage went on strike, stopped dead and pulled back. One of my fingers stuck in the bundle of ropes and it felt as if it had been yanked off. Agony.

Convinced she had broken my finger I called her every name under the sun in several languages and left her to follow, or not, while I nursed my hand and poured whiskey from my leather "bota" hanging on the saddle down my throat and all over the finger. Not sure how I thought this would help but it seemed a good idea at the time. Pretty as a picture, and sensing that she had fallen from grace, Bruma then followed close behind us the rest of the way.

We skirted the village of Domingo Perez which Penelope described as *"the lost village"* because it hides in a little hollow, coming into view at the last minute.

*

A couple of months earlier I had ventured into the narrow streets with José Eduardo, our mission to see if we could find somewhere for the horses and me to stay. I followed him into the tobacconists where astonished ladies in the Spanish equivalent of twin set and pearls (patterned blouses with bosom room and serious earrings) were shaking their heads. Horses? B&B? No ideas. Leaving the shop we met a plumber and a couple of his cronies. After long discussion it was decided that the only people nowadays who knew anything about "bestias" (that includes horses, donkeys, mules and jennets) were the gypsies, so we walked down the steep streets to their part of town, looking for Pinocho or Antonio Tomas. Everywhere was apparently deserted apart from a woman who was either simple or secretive and was not going to divulge where we could find either Pinocho or Antonio Tomas. I began to feel a tad uncomfortable, looking at the silent, bleak little concrete yards hung with washing and the unfenced olive groves in every direction. I could not see anywhere I would want to leave two horses who had just done over thirty kilometres of trail.

This was my first attempt to find village accommodation and I was glad of José's stalwart presence, though only in Andalusia would you be introduced as "This woman. Look at her! She is sixty-seven and still on a horse, setting out alone to ride across two provinces. How is that for courage?"

I began to feel rather like a dear old mare who was doing very well considering. Only a spoilsport would have pointed out that she was still only sixty-six and three quarters at that time!

Finally we went to the Town Hall where the charming postman told us in which bar to find the even more charming young mayor, Eloy Vera. We discussed various possibilities within the village, none of which were going to work, until finally Eloy, my thirty- something, slim, dark saviour, said the magic words

"Well I have a Cortijo a kilometre out of town with space for the horses and bedrooms..."

So here I was, riding along sandy trails to Eloy Vera's

cortijo "Haza de Dios". He was waiting to welcome us and so was his father, a slightly more rustic and rounded version of his son, both needing firm handshakes from my agonising whiskey-soaked hand.

Leaving the untacked horses grazing, as if they had been starved for a week, among the old bits of machinery scattered around the "cortijo", we went inside to where an olive wood fire was blazing as the evening cooled rapidly. I had lots of questions to ask Eloy and his father, also called Eloy, (this is very common in Andalusia and the source of endless familial muddles on my part) and I wasn't going to be able to hold a pen with my finger, now the size, colour and consistency of a chorizo. So I decided to try out the recorder on my phone. However, though at first we sat quite close together, the immense heat the olive fire gave out meant we gradually had to push our chairs back away from it and from each other and, with the crackling of the fire drowning our increasingly distant voices, the recording wasn't a great success.

Eloy senior remembered very well the time when Penelope would have ridden through.

"It was all animals then, no machines at all. I remember the animals were kept in the courtyards of the houses and led through the house every day. Everyone was very poor. A daily worker made 50 or 60 pesetas (less than half a Euro), which nobody could live on and it was around then people started emigrating. They went to Northern Spain, Germany, Switzerland. You see there were two thousand people in the village in 1960, now there are about nine hundred. People had such big families and there just wasn't work for everyone. I knew at least two families who had fifteen kids."

However, Domingo Perez did better than many other villages because in 1959 the agrarian law was enforced and the lord and owner of all the lands around, the Marques de Albayda, started selling off plots to the villagers who up until then had been his tenants. Everyone who could, obtained a bank loan and bought their own few hectares. Some of those that had emigrated came home with enough money to add to their family's "finca" or farmland. Once they were landowners, things started looking up and they worked together, neighbours helping each other at the busy times of year to weed their crops, harvest with scythes, and plough with shared mules. As the olive planting increased, there were trees to prune and fruit to gather in nets.

Eloy senior reckoned it was olives that had lifted the standard of living out of all recognition in two generations.

"We always had a few olives and they do so well here people started planting more and more. Olives were a solution for everyone. Domingo Perez is very lucky for a small village; to this day nearly everyone has their own land and the Co-op helps with that and those who have very few hectares are paid a daily wage to work with those who have more. In the villages that depend on seasonal or daily agricultural work the people cannot survive. They still have to emigrate to the cities."

Is he nostalgic for the old days when the mule trains took the corn to the railhead and everyone kept their own pig to be killed annually?

"Not at all! Those were very hard times. Things are much better for all my children and grandchildren now, and I'm glad."

Eloy junior, as well as being Mayor of Domingo Perez, is

a kindergarten teacher and works their land with his father. I wondered if he wanted his two-year old son to stay in the village or study to move on in the world. He laughed.

"I want him to study and stay!"

What was he most proud of as his achievements as Mayor so far?

"I am the first Mayor of this village. It used to be a dependent of Iznalloz town which is twenty kilometres away. My objective had always been our independence and in 2015 we became our own municipality with a town hall. This means we can control our own grants, permissions, and get funds direct from the province without waiting and arguing over everything with the Mayor of Iznalloz. We have plenty of shops plus a clinic, a library, a sports centre and a bank in Domingo Perez. This has made me proud and satisfied. Everywhere must move on. "

Later, after the Eloys had returned to their houses in the village, I sat in front of the fire with a glass of whiskey, an owl drowning the faint munching of the horses outside. Boiling some water, I poured it on the first of my dehydrated meals – British army Thai green curry. Surprisingly delicious. Then I climbed into my sleeping bag and dangled my right hand in a bucket of cold water beside me. Let´s see what the morning brings.

*

April 4th

A vertical climb to the forgotten Drove Road

Waking in the silent "cortijo", I walked out to a perfect morning to find both horses fast asleep on the well-chewed grass. It took me a long time to prepare and load them as adjusting and dipping into the pack paniers with chorizo finger had to be done with care. I was determined to ride Mademoiselle Bruma today to put a stop to her hoof-stamping tantrums which were surely brought on by a lot of high octane oats and spring grass. The Spanish have a saying "A fiddle and a horse are best tuned by their owner". Within one hundred metres of leaving the Cortijo gates she started her shenanigans, absolutely refusing to cross a tiny trickle of water on the track. I broke a stick off a tree and gave her a bit of the ´who began it´ while Luqa stood aside and watched with a mixture of bemusement and embarrassment, as blokes do when their womenfolk argue.

I won the argument and for the rest of our journey, although she often took flying leaps over damp places and mud puddles, she never stopped dead and dug her toes in again.

We rode through what I now knew to be the prosperous little village of Domingo Perez and out past a few "aldeas" in an easterly direction. "Aldeas" are overgrown farms that have become almost hamlets with outbuildings and dwellings around a central courtyard. Once multiple families lived and grew and worked in them and they still have a charm and a feeling of importance in the landscape. Most, however, now just house the tools of modern agriculture: tractors and trailers and machines to shake the fruit out of olive trees, ploughs and spraying tanks. The windows of the little houses nestling up against the big barns and spreading stables are blind and empty, and snapdragons and wild roses grow out of the roofs. Ironically, many of these deserted hamlets bear the name "Aldea Nueva", or New Aldea, telling us how once they were vibrant and shipshape, something to be proud of. Gradually our little paved lane gave way to dirt tracks leading to open country and, for the first time ever, I switched my phone onto a Wikiloc trail. This route had been drawn for me by José Eduardo, a direct traverse of about ten kilometres of olive groves to cross a main road and link with the old mule trail to Torre Cardela. Over the last four days I had been following what I could ascertain of Penelope´s route from her book almost exactly but was out of sync. with her as I did not stay the first night in Moclín, and so my overnight stops did not coincide with hers. When you are riding a horse, daily distances become fairly precise and an extra five or six kilometres after a full day´s ride is not an option, nor is stopping after only half a day just to stay in one of Penelope´s villages. The route I took this sunny morning she had ridden in the afternoon, getting quite badly lost.

I wonder why nobody has yet invented "devices" with screens that are clearly visible in the open air and in sunshine – and possibly to half-blind old ladies without their specs. I had, at extraordinary expense, invested in a pair of those reading glasses that you wear around your neck and clip together in front with a magnet. I thought they would be ideal for easy accessibility on the horses. Not so. Have you ever tried to ride and lead two horses and click the specs together over the bridge of your nose with one hand? So with a horse in each hand and the phone buried in a pocket, I soon learnt to follow Wikiloc by sound. When I passed a turning I should have taken or strayed too far off the designated route, it made an irritated "Wah wah", so back we went to try again. Once the right track was regained, it chirruped at me encouragingly. Over the many days of riding I only used this method of finding my way very occasionally but even then the horses learned how it worked. By the time I had used it twice, they both ground to a halt whenever the "wah wah" emerged from my pocket, knowing a change of direction was required, and seemed as relieved as I was when it gave us a go-ahead chirrup.

After about two hours the track swung south and my phone objected. Straight ahead to the east was a steep wall of olive terraces, high and practically sheer. I don't think José Eduardo had studied the contour lines when he drew my route. Back and forth we rode, trying to find a way round the great ascent, to no avail. Finally I decided to give it a go with my mountaineering mare but, rather as I feared, Luqa on his lead rope couldn't believe I was serious and nearly pulled me off backwards at each attempt. In the end I unclipped his lead and left him. We had to get a good speed up to make it and I lay along Bruma's neck holding onto her mane just behind her ears as she scrambled and zig-zagged her way up the sheer hillside. Eventually we reached the top and I heard dismal frantic whinnies coming from far below us as Luqa pleaded with us to come back. I was relying on the fact that I had not yet seen any other livestock around today, let alone horses, to make the Hispano-Arab gelding lonesome enough to follow us up. As Penelope had done in these same hills so long ago I had a word with the Man Upstairs and sure enough, after what seemed an age, up Luqa came, crashing through the last few olives and leaving one of the nosebags that had been hanging from his pack somewhere on the way up. No way was I going back to look for it.

On the other side of the hill, far below us, was a deep "barranco" and it rang a bell. That must have been the "gully" where Penelope writes of being lost. She did not come up the hill as I did but continued lower down and ended up following the barranco.

"My track turned bang south. I took my bearings and knew that I should go straight ahead where there was a hill at right angles to the ground. So I turned and rode northwards along an indistinct track...which wound in and out of a gully between steep hills, the tops of which were ploughed. But it was evening and the plough-men had all gone home with their dogs and their mules and there was not even a bird to be seen or heard. The sun kept dodging about all around us as we wound our worried way through the silent deserted gully for we were completely lost...It was getting towards sundown and I began to think we should have to spend the night in this valley of the dead... Then I knelt down, squashed between

40

thorn bushes, and prayed to the Blessed Virgin to help us, pointing out that it was evidently too big a task for St. Christopher whose rightful province it was to look after travellers. I looked up and noticed that the almost perpendicular hill above us was ploughed to halfway down. I started to scramble up it on all fours, pulling the mare behind me. By superhuman efforts we reached the plough level and then plodded our way up to the top of the hill. About a kilometre to the south-east stood a large white farmhouse. No shipwrecked sailor was ever more thankful to see a sail"

From my perch far above Penelope's gully I could imagine her and the Marquesa struggling up through the heavy plough, now olive groves, and I knew she must have come up the other side of the very same hill I had climbed because I could also see the white farmhouse standing beside the road which we both had to cross to reach Torre Cardela.

Alas, when I reached the farmhouse there was no woman in the doorway to point us the way as she did to Penelope. Only ghosts inhabited the empty courtyard, and the broken archway over the rotting door was hidden in honeysuckle and vines that once shaded the pergola from the hot sunshine of another era.

The minor road is now major (large road signs and crash barriers) and the mule trail to the next village, still a rolling, curving, climbing journey but widened and paved. On one side, the stone-faced banks which cradled the ancient way remain and, on the other side, heaps of rock dumped high and heavy by tractors, instead of dry stone walls. In three days riding across these plains, crowded with olives and not much else, I had found many of the bohreens unexpectedly tarmacked. They are still deserted and picturesque and one wonders who bothered to pave them. While riding along this nine kilometre stretch, unable to get off the hard surface because of the walls of stone on either side, I met not one single vehicle. There were several beautiful but deserted "cortijos" along my way, all with large roadside troughs for passing animals to drink from, usually situated on very green grass where there was obviously a spring. Sadly they were all dry, the water rerouted to the demanding, spoiled olives. It was hot and I began to feel for my thirsty steeds who hadn't had a drink since before they climbed their Everest a few hours earlier. Along that winding stretch of lane I counted seven empty stone water troughs where the Marquesa and others could have drunk their fill in 1961. I found an open farmyard gate with an idling tractor inside and asked the driver for water. He was very apologetic but all the water in the tank in the yard had already had some noxious chemical added to it for fumigating the olive groves, and he had no more ideas except to ride on to Torre Cardela where there was a drinking trough to which he directed me.

Penelope described the sunset as she rode towards her destination as the most glorious afterglow she had seen since leaving Delhi. She was the daughter of Field Marshall Lord Chetwode, a high-ranking cavalry officer stationed in India where she spent her years as a young woman, so she was no stranger to hard riding across rough country and beautiful sunsets. Taking advantage of the so-called "cold weathers" in India, during her late teens and twenties, Penelope, accompanied by her mother, Star Chetwode, went on riding expeditions. They explored the foothills of the Himalayas and it was then that her abiding love for India was born. A love that drew her back, long after her Andalusian adventure, to lead treks across that magical sub-continent and further her knowledge and love of Indian art and history.

When she arrived in the village of Torre Cardela the "posada" doors were open in welcome and the landlord led La Marquesa to water and then into the huge stable with deep litter on the floor. A few mules and donkeys were tied at the long manger where he served a supper of barley and straw to the weary mare. This was the first of many villages where Penelope found herself the centre of a rather exhausting interest on the part of the children who followed her everywhere, fascinated by this extraordinary stranger. She was served broth with saffron and fresh sardines for supper, eating with a young pedlar who sold goods from his donkey and a cave dweller from Guadix selling shirts and socks from his motorbike.

The main road running through the village, which I crossed as I led the horses to the very trough the Marquesa was taken to, is busy now with tractors and trucks, the latter travelling at a speed the young hawker on his donkey could not have imagined. Before she left the next morning, Penelope went to mass in the parish church where the priest's dog also attended. This did not seem to be an unusual occurrence in Andalusia then, as she mentions while describing one of the first masses she went to in Spain.

"Antonio had a little rough haired terrier on short legs, the shape of a small Corgi, of which he was as fond as the most ardent English dog-lover. One night I went to evening devotions in the big church across the plaza. I arrived late and fell flat across the corner of the confessional which set a whole pew of children off into a fit of giggles. Then Chico came in, singled me out as his master's friend and came and lay down at my feet. The Blessed Sacrament was exposed and instead of letting a sleeping dog lie quite innocently in

*the Divine Presence I got up and carried him out. On returning to
my place I again fell flat over the confessional. I soon learned that it
was the usual thing for dogs to wander in and out of church in Spain
and that nobody minded. Many priests have dogs who regularly
hear mass sitting motionless in an aisle with apparent devotion."*

When she told the priest at Torre Cardela that she had left
her rosary under her pillow at Santo Domingo and wished to
buy another, he took one out of his pocket and gave it to her
which touched her greatly.

After my horses had drunk, with a lot of blowing bubbles
and snorting and plunging noses in up to their eyes in satisfaction, I asked where the "posada" had been and was shown a
little modern shop that stood where the old building had been
pulled down. I led them further up the road to the plain white
church where Penelope had gone to Mass. It was locked, as,
I was to discover, are many church buildings containing anything of value and near a main road, and services are normally
just twice a week, unlike the twice or even thrice daily communions of sixty years ago.

Penelope left Torre Cardela with the whole village gathered to bid her farewell.

My departure was a lot more low key. She had decided in
what she describes as a "cowardly way" to stick to the metalled
road all the way to Pedro Martinez but I had spotted what I
thought might be a "cañada" on the map and wanted to try and
go that way. "Cañadas", - pronounced canyarda , not Canada -
are the old drove roads that were used for livestock movement
and long distance trade all over Spain. They are supposedly
protected and the many "Cañada Reales" belong to the King.
They should be maintained many metres wide to allow large

flocks and herds to progress along them and it is forbidden to close them off in any way. However, inevitably, in areas like the one I was riding through where no large animals seem to exist, let alone need to be taken anywhere cross country, land-owners will put up wire fences across "cañadas", or they get overgrown beyond recognition, or suburbs of bigger towns encroach on them and the rights of passage are ignored. As the horses and I walked through the little alleyways at the back of Torre Cardela, I met a man in his seventies and asked him about the "cañada" I was seeking. He flatly denied its existence but I carried on looking.

About ten minutes later, after a few dead ends, I was retrac-ing my steps when I met him again, this time with a committee of old gentlemen who had obviously been discussing my re-quest. Just two of them remembered that there was a "cañada" and only one of them knew where it was. Thus has tradition died out in such a short time in these parts. So a little procession of us walked slowly to the outskirts of town and I was put on the right road, a beautiful grassy sandy track between arable fields with wheat and barley dancing in the breeze, where Penelope, in November, would have seen plough. My send-off committee had become more animated as I told them my plans and they began remembering their parents´ and grandpar-ents´ beasts of burden, their names and eccentricities. There was Toto the mule who thought he was a dog, Acebuche the handsome stallion and Lola the much beloved donkey mare who taught a little boy to ride. So we stood and chatted in the breezy sunshine and their faces cracked in reminiscent grins as they patted Luqa and Bruma, discussing their shiny coats and well-filled bellies. Then they started to recall talk of the visit of the foreign woman who stayed a night with her mare in the posada, but none of them had actually seen her, though some of their school friends had been lucky enough to be there. I got the feeling none of these fellows wanted me to leave, bringing, as I did, a link with the rare old days.

The afternoon ride was beautiful. I was at one with Penelope who wrote how "...*these trails, with their alluringly sinuous ways, are gravely tempting me to go riding along them forever.*" We passed over streams between rolling fields of crops and poppies and by some prosperous "aldeas", newly painted and filled with cottages and outbuildings, bustling with life as they should be. We even saw some sheep! A first since I left Ronda.

However my "cañada" came to a sticky end when we tried to cross the railway. I reached the part near the old fashioned station where Penelope met a man in a grey peaked railway uniform cap leading the little railway delivery donkey, laden with packages, but it was firmly fenced off. When I tried to cross further along the line the tracks had a deep concrete pit running under the rails, impassable with the horses. So we were back on the road.

There are thirteen kilometres altogether between the two villages and it seemed ten more in the heat of the afternoon once I was back on the tarmac. There had been a plan that Juan Antonio Fernandez, Mayor of Pedro Martinez, and his friend would ride out to meet me but there was no sign of anyone as we crossed the treeless plain. It was riding along here that Penelope saw the first tractors of her trip. *"I was disgusted"* she wrote, uncompromisingly.

We were banjaxed by the time we reached Pedro Martinez

in the early evening and I called the mayor but he simply wasn´t picking up his phone. I rode into town past another dry trough where the Marquesa had had the good fortune to find water, and asked the way to the Mayor´s "finca" or farm where he had promised me horse accommodation. As if we hadn´t enough annoyance, it turned out that Juan Antonio is something of a local tycoon and has several "fincas". I was directed to one out near the cemetery and, although it looked unlikely that there was a place for horses there, I decided to tie up outside and let the horses graze until I could raise Juan Antonio on the phone. Eventually he spotted all the missed calls which he hadn´t heard on board his noisy tractor.

He arrived at top speed in a smart 4 x 4, a generously circular fellow with a beaming smile accompanied by his elegantly upholstered wife without the beaming smile. He showed me where to take the horses a little way back to the correct "cortijo" where they had beautiful big stables and all the hay they needed for both feed and bedding. In the third stable was a dog who never stopped barking and couldn´t see out, so I threw picnic remains over the door to shut it up. Over the next three days that invisible dog got quite a lot of strange sustenance which probably gave it the most frightful tummy ache if it was only used to dog biscuit but it gave the horses and me a little respite to gather our thoughts for a think!

My accommodation was at the far end of town, a house of nerve-wracking cleanliness run by Doña Gertrudis, the only place to stay in town. I arrived feeling slightly sheepish with all my bundles and bags to which was attached quite a lot of vegetation and she immediately took me to the washing machine in the utility room. This was actually a really wonderful idea as I was due to stay here two nights – what an opportunity! Then she showed me my room.

I was too weary to go out and find a bar for supper so the British Army and I got up close and personal again – this time goulash.

I went to bed a happy woman as, after a hot shower, I could detect a very faint bend in chorizo finger.

Top: The old Cañada. Below: The Mayor of Pedro Martinez reading a letter Karen brought from the Mayor of Gaucin

April 5th

Remembering Paloma

A day's rest was welcome for the horses' backs and legs and my head. Like Penelope I needed to catch up on my journal, look at maps and talk to people. Unlike Penelope I was also fielding Whatsapp, email and writing a daily Instagram, none of which, due to my incredibly clumsy fingers and screen blindness, I could even attempt when I was actually on the horses.

Doña Gertrudis' establishment is a couple of kilometres from Mayor Juan Antonio's "finca" and I strode out under cloudy morning skies with a nippy little wind blowing down from the great wall of the Sierra Nevada. The weather was on the change. I was glad Luqa and Bruma were sheltered in their echoey stables, though, what with the continuously barking dog and bold Bruma making a show of herself shouting flirtatiously to the Mayor's stallion in a paddock a few hundred metres away, it was scarcely peaceful. Luqa definitely had bags under his eyes - but was pleased to see his breakfast.

With no need to rush, I had a chance to look around the relatively newly-built establishment where they were housed. Isn't it extraordinary how empty spaces fill up with things when you are not looking? This is a phenomenon I recognise from Irish farmyards. There were stacks of wood, pallets, empty and full oil cans, garden furniture, kitchen chairs, assorted ironmongery, piles of stones, barrels and pot plants, a box of boots and shoes, a tin hat from Franco's era, an ancient tractor, three attached dogs and a vast antediluvian combine harvester. I knew the only reason I had found my allotted stables empty was because those dogs had been in them until just before I arrived. It goes without saying that, in spite of such a cornucopia of stuff, I couldn't find a fork or a shovel, a barrow or a bucket anywhere!

I think Penelope's system of just riding into the villages unannounced fitted well with the Andalusian way. If I announced my arrival a week ahead, the answer was always the same.

"No te preocupes" which immediately meant I was pre-occupied because I knew they had not yet given it a thought! Generally speaking, when I was a couple of days away, stables were cleared, my accommodation sorted and my arrival not a huge surprise. However, Penelope had the advantage of pretty well guaranteed lodging for herself and her mount in the "posadas" of the day, while I had to prepare something in advance or run the risk of finding the three of us in the street; though the people are so kind that probably would never happen. Yet even the two hour wait yesterday, after seven hours in the saddle, had seemed interminable. One rides the last couple of kilometres anticipating arriving, unpacking, untacking, feed and hay and water for the deserving horses (and then a bar and a shower for oneself, not necessarily in that order. Bliss.). So when that doesn´t happen quite as soon as you´d imagined, it seems like a long delay.

As the promised rain came thundering down, I had an appointment at the Town Hall with the jolly round Mayor and José Antonio Lopez who was born in Pedro Martinez in 1945 and has worked for many years for the Town Hall. Jose´s childhood in the 1950´s was during the post-Civil War crisis and he remembered how the village was when Penelope rode through.

"There were five thousand inhabitants of Pedro Martinez then and all we had were the crops and the livestock. We lived hand to mouth, worked dawn to dusk. The tracks were full of workers travelling to and from the land on mules, on donkeys, on foot, occasionally on bicycles, to do the seasonal work that was necessary. The land was harrowed or ploughed, weeded and prepared and then the seed cast by hand - great arcs of it - more weeding to protect the crops, harvesting with scythes, and finally the gathering and storing of the grain. This was milled to flour for our own bread, the surplus sold on by the state. We had four hectares of paved threshing floors alone for our grain. In summer they were completely filled with whole families taking part in the many activities necessary for the harvest. Men came from Almeria to help harvest and thresh the grain because we were a land-rich village, and still are, with fourteen thousand hectares, most of it arable. Whole groups of them came, so thin and barefoot. We called Almeria the land of three harvests, esparto grass, flies and sickness. They were poorer than us, they had nothing. Of course now they have the "invernaderos" (fruit and veg growing under plastic) and tourism."

Esparto grass grows wild and used to be gathered in all the villages to make the ropes and cords in everyday use, the mats for the olive presses and to weave into baskets and containers of all sorts. Now, it is collected by people who need the work and the village of Pedro Martinez has a grant to ensure a respectable wage to them for their harvest. When plastic is banned, who knows, esparto may well come into its own again.

José Antonio told me of the huge flocks of sheep and herds of goats that filled the meadows and "cañadas" then, and of one José Rufino who walked his animals to the mountains of Cazorla every year when grazing became sparse. I was to see what a long and complicated route that was when I rode it over the next week.

"When I was a boy everything we did was by hand or with animals, often combining our mule with our neighbour´s so then we had a team for ploughing. My parents sowed and weeded and harvested, carefully keeping good seed corn to use again the following year"

What would his parents have wished for their children?

"They would not have thought ahead, it was all about keeping the family, working to eat. There were no real ambitions then but in the late 1950´s, when the Marquesa de Heredia´s lands in plots of three hectares came up for sale, it was the saving of some of the poorest families. They then had their own little bit of soil to cultivate."

He talked fondly of his childhood in the village, remembering the games they played, many of which I could not translate though some I recognised, such as football, cops and robbers with homemade wooden pistols, spinning tops and rolling hoops for the boys. The girls had skipping ropes and hula hoops and played dolls "without the dolls". Would he like to go back to those times?

"No, life was a great deal more difficult than it is now."

In the early 60´s emigration had started and the menfolk and then whole families were leaving to go to Cataluña, the Basque country and Germany where they were welcomed as guest workers. The population started to drop then and now stands at about twelve hundred. It was at the beginning of this exodus that Penelope rode through the village.

She wrote of Pedro Martinez as a perfect example of the pueblos of that era. She loved the way everything had grown over time, the cobbled streets, white-washed stone walls and little courtyards where old ladies in black sewed while children played. She compared the Spanish pueblo very favourably with English villages where she believed this homogenous quality had been lost when "progress" marched in.

"I was so transported by the harmony of the whole pattern – people, houses, mules, donkeys, tiles and tassels – that I wished those minutes could have been years."

Well, progress has marched in to Pedro Martinez now - in particular concrete! The centre is still mainly narrow white streets, apart from the modern church and Town Hall and a few ill-advised "renovations", but the approach from every direction is marred, to my eyes anyway, by new and often partly-finished houses, all inexplicably huge and many apparently empty. Instead of the curving white walls, soft tiling and imperfect corners of the older houses, these new additions seem vast and give a sort of liquorice allsorts effect: blocks of odd colours piled up with unrelenting lines, horizontal slabs of brick, half-finished bilious yellow tiling, and quantities of raw cement. It is as if generations of living in two or three rooms with low doors and few windows has bred a species of giants. A wealth of fancy wrought ironwork on massive doors and windows adds to the feeling of the old village being surrounded and overpowered by aliens.

I asked the Mayor, if the population has dropped to a fifth of the size it was sixty years ago, why is the village now so much bigger?

"Many of those new houses belong to the people who had to emigrate to Barcelona and Palma de Mallorca. They still come back for the summer and for all the fiestas."

A perfect example of how Spanish people are so rooted and families hang together to the third and fourth generation.

Having realised that the Mayor was something of a local tycoon, I was intrigued to find out how he got there.

"My grandfather started a tile-making factory just below where you have the horses. Both my grandfathers had animals and my father went as a "mulero", mule man, at a big "cortijo", working with as many as ten pairs as there was a lot of land. The first tractor to arrive belonged to the co-operative. They had a meeting and decided they could afford one in about 1960. Then came another, privately owned, so this village had two tractors".

Almost certainly those that annoyed Penelope on her way here.

"The transition happened in my father´s lifetime," Juan Antonio continued. "I often think if only my grandfather could see me now. When I was seven or eight I used to go with him to help plough with his mules and now I just sit up on my tractor and cover hectares he wouldn't have dreamed of. To begin with, my father was a day worker, if he didn't work, no pay, but then he became a land surveyor which was a step up. My mother told me how hungry they all were during the Civil War. As a child she once raced another in the street for a bit of orange peel they spotted and the other kid hit her so hard on the head she still has the scar. After the War, her father was locked up in Guadix jail because he was a "Rojo" (Red or Republican) sergeant, and my mother and her sister and my grandmother used to go begging to the "cortijos" for food for him. All they gave them to eat in jail was bread and onions and he couldn't stand onions for the rest of his life!"

Juan Antonio is one of the very few people I have met so far on my journey that has horses. How did that start?

"That began with a little white donkey that belonged to my neighbours. I used to rush home from school so I could load her with the "cantaros", jump on her back and go and fetch the water from the village fountain. Her owner had a cow and the donkey used to carry the milk, all on her own, from the "finca" to the village too. Her name was Paloma. I loved that donkey and then one day, with me at the fountain, she dropped dead. Everyone explained that she was nearly forty years old and it was what happened to old donkeys but I was inconsolable. I cried for days. The neighbour got another but it was black and I was not comforted! We didn't get running water until 1976 when, with the help of a geologist, we sunk a well outside the village and piped it in.

At nineteen I became self-employed and, as soon as I could, I bought a horse. When I was twenty-four I started the bar I still have, and in 2000 I began buying land. By 2006 I had masses of hay and I was selling it all to equestrian centres and the Legion of Cavalry in Almeria. I had about twenty horses myself at that time. Now I have my pure-bred stallion and another gelding and I would never, ever sell them, even though I hardly ever have time to ride them."

In the cold afternoon I returned to the stables carrying some of the clobber from my digs that I could do without. The forecast for my destination next day, Villanueva de las Torres, known in Penelope´s time as "Don Diego", looked a whole lot better in the morning than in the afternoon. I wanted to make an early start, so I couldn´t be too laden down on the necessary walk I would have to take to the horses. They got plenty more feed and hay as the Sierra Nevada range was obscured from view in a white-out and I could smell the snow.

The time had come for a warm bar, a large drink and a delicious plate of something nourishing. I found a very noisy, packed establishment near the centre of town where I had the sort of meal Penelope would have totally recognised. First a bowl of steaming "puchero" a thick soup that involves pork broth and chick peas and all sorts of goodies depending on what the cook has to hand. In the family houses it was served in one bowl and everybody had their own spoon and shared. Then a sizzling plate of cured ham and fried eggs with very yellow yolks. Penelope, when she set out on her travels, often asked her hosts to fry the cured ham and I wonder if she had been told as a little girl, as I was, that undercooked pork gave you worms! Worst of all we were meant to leave the rinds off a rasher of bacon for this reason which was so disappointing as it was the best bit. However, as her tour progressed she seems to have started eating the ham as it arrived. It is such a staple of Andalusia and so delicious, I am glad she tried it ´au naturel´ in the end.

Returning from the village in the sleety rain on my way back to Gertrudis, peering out from under my voluminous mackintosh cape, I found the large threshing floor which Penelope at first thought was an outsized, cobbled, parade ground. Here she was thrilled to see, for the first time, twenty ricks of esparto grass, tied in bundles with a little snow-white donkey working away to build the last rick with her jennet foal at foot. I like to think it might have been Paloma.

＊

April 6th

Down through the blizzard to the Troglodytes

I stepped out of Doña Gertrudis' Casa Rural in the dark early morning and recoiled back inside, slamming the door on the blizzard whipping up the street. When I emerged again, I was wearing two pairs of socks, two shirts, two pairs of trousers, a sweater and a fleece, two scarves, my waterproof Andalusian cape over the lot and my broad-brimmed hat. My clothes rucksack was completely empty except for a couple of pairs of knickers that I really felt would not help with my body heat.

A thin coating of snow over the rooftops lit my way through the village to the stables. I would like to think I looked like Zorro, striding through the silent streets as the snow fell, but it is hard to look dashing when the layers of clothes you have on seriously restrict your movement. I kept falling over the hem of my mac, all the bags and bundles I was carrying preventing me from hitching it up curbs and steps. It seemed a long way to the horses and preparing them took ages as I was juggling to try and prevent us all setting off covered in snow. I did remember to turn my sheepskin on top of the saddle skin side up so the wool wouldn't get saturated but the paniers got snowed into because I kept forgetting to close them after every piece of luggage.

Eventually we were ready and I walked the horses to the gates, closed the padlock, pocketed the precious key and found a tree trunk to get on board from - the two pairs of trousers made mounting even more difficult than usual with Luqa jogging and pulling in the chill wind. So we set off up the little road into the village...and I realised I had left my blinking specs back at the stable. Replay all the above.

We left the key at the Mayor's bar where his beautiful, stout daughter was serving a great many glasses of Anis and Coñac to snowy customers, dodged the Saturday market selling, as far as I could see, mainly Sevillana CD's and enormous bras, and surreptitiously pulled yellow daisies out of Bruma's mouth which she had managed to snatch en route. What is it with the yellow daisies? In the centre of town on a narrow street, an enormous bus appeared through the blizzard ahead at the same time as a very noisy tractor tried to pass us from behind. As far as Luqa was concerned, this was the stuff of nightmares and it took us some time to extricate ourselves from the situation. At last we left the town behind and took a track across the altiplano, Bruma happily chewing on an enormous mouthful of geraniums she must have whipped out of a window box when Luqa was having his conniptions.

The snow was stopping and the Sierra Nevada appeared out of the grey light like a huge lump of icing. The wind seemed to get colder as day broke. I remembered Penelope talking a lot about that icy wind, and it did feel as if it might freeze us solid. We crossed rolling arable land scattered with beautiful but ruined "cortijos" behind whose walls we took brief respite out of the wind. Most were used as stores for agricultural machinery and there were a few workers´ cars around. The labourers of the 21st century choose to come out to work the land daily and return to a cosy little house in one of the villages to live. I could totally sympathise as we struggled through the bitter gusts across the high plain. A modern house with heating and a telly seemed like nirvana.

It was while she rode this track, in less foul weather, that Penelope met donkeys laden with esparto grass and then more donkeys and mules carrying fir branches for the bakers´ ovens. She was a keen photographer and one of her aims was to take transparencies which she could later present as a slide show to accompany a lecture about her travels for the Womens´ Institute, that stalwart body of women that still thrives in Britain. Having learnt the word of command from the gypsy guide who took her and her friends across the Serrania de Ronda, she jumped off her mare and said "Brrrrrrr" and all the mules stopped dead, giving her the chance to take pictures of them and the muleteers.

After I had finished writing this book, I heard from Penelope´s granddaughter, Imogen Lycett Green, that she had recently donated all her grandmother's papers to the British Library where library staff were currently cataloguing the twenty boxes. Her notebooks, manuscripts and photographs will be available for all students of India and Spain worldwide to see and use for research, forever.

At last we left the green, cropped fields and started to drop down into scattered umbrella pine trees or stone pines as Penelope called them, where the bakers´ fuel had come from. The first trees we had seen this morning. By this time I had succeeded in extricating my ancient woollen poncho from its special bag on the back of the saddle and put it on as yet another layer over all my other garments. Now there was no way I was dismounting before our destination, all ideas of a snack or lunch were put on hold because the chance of me being able to get back on again in my multiple garments was nil.

Feeling warmer and able to think of something apart from how cold I was (there is a lot of thinking time on these long rides) I hoped the dog in the neighbouring stable in Pedro Martinez had enjoyed his breakfast of leftover ham and bread with garlic. This led me to wondering how it would have been if I had brought my own dog along on the adventure. I had recently obtained, after an awful lot of Cava on flamenco night in the village, an Australian Shepherd, though I prefer to call him a collie, a shepherd for me is a handsome mountainy bloke with a crook. Rory was not at all my usual sort of canine, having had generations of naughty, feisty, little hunting terriers, and it was taking me a while to get used to all his fancy colouring and flowing fur – and to forgive myself for being such an eejit as to say yes to him in the first place. However he would follow the horses to the ends of the earth and even round them up in the right direction once in a while to be fed or caught, so I was beginning to realise I had in fact a serious dog in a silly frock. Take away the frilly knickerbockers and fancy ruff and underneath was a working animal. The breed was new to my village when I got him and the neighbours always asked what cross he was. Rory looks like a leopard mated a ballerina! Although he could easily have done the distances, I left him behind on this adventure. Firstly, because it would have been extra weight carrying his food on the pack horse and, secondly, I knew many of the places I was leaving the horses would almost certainly have their own dogs who would not welcome an outsider. Thirdly, if we did have to ride along main roads, it would just be another worry. I know I made the right decision.

After we passed a particularly beautiful and ghostly "aldea" called La Cardera we started to descend on an old trail. Things began looking up, the older the trail, the better the shelter and the kinder the contours. We were dropping into the spectacular gorge, like a huge fault in the earth, that runs north across Granada Province from Guadix. An extraordinary lunar landscape opened up beneath us to the east and north as we zigzagged down between the pink and rose-red cliffs. We lost the wind which was a blessed relief, however, I could now see that the Sierra Cazorla, where I would be headed in a couple of days, was also covered in snow – April how are you?

The terrain was stony and exciting with big drops on either side and the horses walked with care until, suddenly, they stopped and four ears pointed at a spot on the mountainside below us. Luqa whinnied loud and long and an answer echoed up to us. There was a small herd of mares and youngsters clustered on the top of a hummock, glossy and fat. They watched as we approached, then circled us a couple of times as my horses looked on, agog and trembling, until the lead mare turned with a flick of her tail and a kick of her heels and led the others away at the gallop around a rocky shoulder of mountain and they were lost to view, like a dream. They looked so well on gorse and thyme and stones which was the only fodder I could see in the multi-coloured canyon.

As we continued down towards Villanueva de las Torres, the first evidence of the cave houses appeared, pipes coming out of the mountains which were the chimneys of the caves below. In Penelope's time, this village was known as "Don Diego", although even then she says that was not the name on the map. Don Diego himself had been the lord of the village to whom everyone gave a chicken a year in rental. I knew what I was coming to but Penelope, arriving after dark, found it all a very dramatic experience.

"The stony road wound down in a series of hairpin bends and soon we were enveloped in the blanket of the moonless night. I got off and led the Marquesa because I thought she might inadvertently step over a precipice... something unpleasant must be lurking in the inky depths of those ravines to pounce on us. Then, without any warning at all, there appeared a hundred holes with lights in them in the middle of the shadowy hills, and the screams of demons filled the night.

I had come upon a colony of troglodytes"

My arrival in daylight was less spectacular but it was still akin to descending to another world where the faery folk dig and delve, far from dwellers of the high plains and the roaring winds.

Twenty-four hours earlier, I had called Paco who was hosting my horses, to say I hoped to arrive around lunchtime and he had said "No te preocupes" – so of course he wasn't there. He had gone in his car by road to Pedro Martinez on an errand. I found the brick shed where he keeps his stallion with a huge cave stable behind. He also has a little paddock up against a rock face at the back but, as it was beginning to rain hard, I put both the horses in the stable where they were cosy and happy and Bruma could flirt with Paco's stallion next door through the wall. There was a lovely atmosphere about the place and when Paco turned up with a load of hay, I realised he creates that atmosphere around him. Middle aged, with a solemn smile and well-worked hands, he had prepared his second stable beautifully for us with water laid on and somewhere to store my equipment. He introduced me to his much-loved stallion, Lucero, who was looking stunning, huge and shiny.

"I lost a mare to colic so I never give him any grain, just hay or grass"

Ah bollix! I had been planning on donating a sack of wonderful mixed oats to him. I had overestimated horse feed and did not want to carry extra weight on with me.

A friend of his, Manuel, a little older, arrived and helped to unload the hay. He told me proudly that he also had horses. The rain increased from persistent to lashing but it didn't matter now. Bruma and Luqa were safe and warm.

Paco works in the campo with two thousand of his own olive trees to tend plus one hundred and twenty hectares of olives and almonds which he manages for another owner. On behalf of the owner he employs two permanent men and can usually give work to four or five or more. In the harvesting season and at busy times he takes on more workers paid by the day. Even flat out with all those people, he told me, the olive and almond harvest for both properties takes over sixty days. All of which leaves him very little time to ride the horse he dotes on though his little dog, Cuqui, who goes everywhere with him, spends time playing games with the lovely gentle horse in his box.

Pepe Vallejo, the Mayor of Villanueva de las Torres, turned up in his car at this point. Hugely helpful, from the first day I got in touch with him, he is a neat man, a young grandfather, impeccable in V-necked sweater, shirt and cord trousers. Brought up in one of the outlying "aldeas", he makes sure that every visitor to his town is looked after like family and, when I gave him the translation of Penelope's time in Don Diego he started reading it there and then. I climbed in his car out of the rain and he took me to the lodging he had found for me as there was nowhere at all taking guests in the village. This used to be a Casa Rural but the owner, Doña Enriqueta, had closed it, I suspect because she didn't like it getting dirty. She had been persuaded to open up just for me and the poor woman definitely regretted her decision when this weather-beaten ould one, wearing an extraordinary layering of clothes came to her door carrying most of the stable in her poncho plus quantities of mixed bags, all sodden with melting snow. She offered me the very smallest of the available rooms, obviously with a view to corralling the filth and legged it back up the shiny, sterile staircase to the safety of her own plague-free quarters.

Pepe then gave me a lift to the bar in the centre of town where I planned on having a very late lunch. I tried what was to become a staple of mine when I was really hungry "Hamburguesa Completa". An Iberian version of the "Full Irish" served in a crusty bun from the local bakery, it involves two eggs, bacon, onions, white pudding, black pudding, tomato, lettuce and often surprise extras like anchovies or artichokes! I suppose there is a little burger of some sort in there but I have never noticed!

On this rainy Saturday afternoon at every table in the bar except mine, a rattling, clacking, shouting game of dominos was going on, with four or six contestants at each. I remembered a photo in Penelope's book of three boys playing dominos in the doorway of one of the cave houses of Villanueva. It was beautifully taken against the light and one of my favourites of hers. Finding the page (and the courage) I circulated, interrupting the furious games to show each table the photo. Finally one man of about seventy did a double take and said, "That's me!" pointing at one of the kids in the photo in astonishment.

Well, I wrecked that game for the next half an hour as all the players helped remember who the other two boys were and then they started to reminisce about Penelope's visit. She stayed four days in their village so most of the children who were there at that time had known about her, if not seen her. They reiterated the phrase "Una Señora sola", a lady alone, which was what had struck them most forcibly. The remaining two boys in the photo had emigrated with their families to Barcelona and Mallorca which seems to be something I would come up against everywhere as I searched for the people Penelope knew. However I was much encouraged to have found one person that featured in her book so long ago and he was delighted! Of course important things in daily life must go on, so they went back to their game, but word was out that I was here and what I was looking for which was to help me in my investigations in "Don Diego".

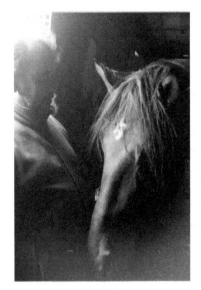

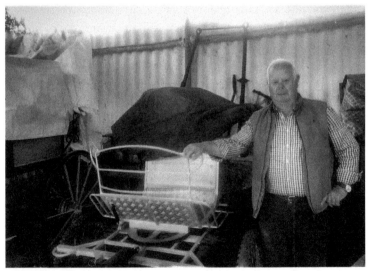

Clockwise from top left: Paco and Lucero, PC's photo of boys playing dominos, Manolo and his carriages.

*

April 7th

Doña Encarna - my birthday treat

My birthday dawned beneath grey skies that threw the white and pink-grey walls of the gorge that holds "Don Diego" in its heart into a magnified, limpid relief. The church where Penelope went to mass was just across the street from my bedroom and the bells clattered noisily, insisting I attend the Sunday service. With a backdrop of the strange lunar hills, the building was exactly as she described it: simple, solid, in an unadorned classical style, whitewashed both inside and out. Because the morning was not particularly warm, the priest and his helpers were trying to light the space heaters which took a while as they were having wick trouble, but warmed us up nicely in the end. Penelope remarked how the service sheets were printed out in phonetic Latin which she found most extraordinary. This was to try and get everyone to join in the responses but only the younger girls, the little boy serving the mass and she herself opened their mouths. It was obvious that most of the congregation could not read.

As far as I could tell everyone in church this Sunday morning in 2019 could read and even sing the responses very nicely, and men and women were no longer segregated to sit on opposite sides of the church, which is something else she mentions. It seems rather a puritan idea for a little Catholic church, even in the 1960's and not one I have ever heard of. However, we were thin on the ground. Instead of bursting with little catechists the congregation seemed to be made up of people the same age as Penelope would have been had she lived until now – that's one hundred and nine! I lit a candle for my intention of finishing this ride with all three of us in one piece and asked God for his help in my enterprise and then went to tell my two companions that I thought I had got Him on our side.

They were not in a Sabbath mood and shot out of the cave stable when I opened the door to roll luxuriously in the rain-soaked, treacle-brown shit rivulets draining from Paco's dung heap into the little sand paddock, getting up and then throwing themselves down again onto alternating shoulders to really grind in the muck. Then they stood side by side, stinky and dripping, and demanded breakfast.

I was dying to find the posada where Penelope had stayed with Rosendo Coral, the landlord, who loved animals so much and had a beautiful mule for whom he cut bundles of Lucerne hay. When they first arrived, he pointed out that La Marquesa had a lump on her belly from a rubbing cinch and helped to cure it, then rubbed hog's lard into the offending girth to soften it. His wife, Carmen, spent a lot of time looking after her delicate little boy, Juan Jesus, who was eight months old and had been born premature and rhesus negative, known then as a "blue baby".

Plenty of corner boys, as we call them at home, were in the streets to tell me the whereabouts of the "posada". Rather than hanging around waiting for the Sunday pubs to open, I felt these lads were waiting for their domino partners to turn up. Yes, some knew which "posada" I meant but it wasn't there anymore, and they directed me to a brand-new pristine bank built on the site of the old building. Hard to get the atmosphere or even to imagine how it must have been when all I could see was my own reflection on the shiny glass and chrome. As I walked away a head popped out of a doorway.

"The lady who wants to know about Penelope?"

This was Juan Valle Martinez, a neighbour of Rosendo and Carmen and family, and father-in-law of Pepe, the mayor. He invited me in and told me how, when he was doing his military service in Granada, he heard that Carmen had had a sickly baby that needed a blood transfusion in the nearby hospital. He walked over from the barracks to see if his blood matched and it did, so it was a transfusion from him that saved the baby's life. Now an elderly man, he looks after his wife who has Alzheimer's. She sat immobile and silent as he talked and I could see how beautiful she must have been. They have three daughters living in the village who help their father and who popped in and out while we were talking.

Juan was born and brought up in the now deserted "aldea" I had passed on my ride down into the gorge, La Cardera.

"It belonged to nine brothers and there were twenty families living there. We children were all like siblings, no one differentiated between cousins and brothers and sisters. We played together and helped with the harvests and the animals.

Carmen, who later married Rosendo, was like a big sister to me. It was a wonderful life for the children but hard to feed everybody. Fifty years ago my wife and I had the opportunity to buy land and a cortijo of three hundred odd hectares in the valley with twenty years to pay, so we left the "aldea" and came down to the village to run the farm. At one point we had four hundred goats."

Juan also knew Caridad, whom Penelope met as a beautiful young woman when she went riding along the little River Fardes that runs below the village. Caridad lived in a cave with her old father and her nephew who she was bringing up, as her sister died two days after he was born. Penelope tied La Marquesa up with their mules and was invited in to eat juicy pomegranates by the open fire. They became great friends during the short time the Englishwoman spent in "Don Diego".

"She is in her eighties now and lives in Barcelona with her children but she comes back for a month or two every year to a house just down there on my street. She is my old friend and we always have a laugh together! She is still a beautiful person".

Next I was invited to see Manolo, whom I met yesterday at the stable, and his family. There I found his wife, Carmela and her mother, Doña Encarna. Tiny and enchanting with sparkling brown eyes, and the bright expectancy of a character from Wind in the Willows, in spite of being nearly ninety-five, her memories of Penelope were crystal clear.

"I remember her arriving, stopping at the posada and dismounting from her horse. She had a hat like yours and enormous saddle bags and she was a tall woman. Nothing ever happened here and her arrival made a huge impression on us all. I was in my thirties then. I remember how we all gathered round to welcome her. She liked it here and wherever she went she had her "court" of children following her"

Doña Encarna beamed at the memories.

Indeed Penelope recounts how her every move was watched, even when she was inside the "posada", with the kids climbing up to peer through the shutters to report: "The woman speaks!", "The woman eats", "The woman writes!"

I passed round the now well-thumbed copy of "Two Middle Aged Ladies" and Doña Encarna and her brother José recognised everyone in the photos of "Don Diego". Encarna was born second of ten children and José second last so there is something of an age difference. José is the bachelor brother and lives alone in the next-door street, bemoaning how empty the houses are now that all his neighbours have moved away, either to nearby towns where there is work or to heaven. Manolo and Carmela have seven children but Carmela admitted that big families like theirs are unusual nowadays. She showed me a photo of the school that was built shortly after Penelope's visit. Then the population of the village was three thousand five hundred, now it is about five hundred. Certainly, although the bars are packed with noisy, cheerful sixty and seventy-year olds, I found no sign of the great gangs of kids that followed Penelope from place to place, though I did find exactly where she had taken photos of groups of them on the smooth slopes of the hills below the myriad cave houses.

"As soon as they put in the transport to secondary school in Guadix, the children became over qualified for this village," Carmela explained. "Then they went and found work in bigger towns and cities and brought up their families there, so there are not many children here now. But nearly all come back for the Feria!" (The annual village celebration)

Feeling like a spring chicken beside Doña Encarna's ninety-five year old youthful twinkle, I mentioned that it was my sixty-seventh birthday and it was decided that a photograph was essential. Encarna insisted I kept my hat on because I reminded her of Penelope in it. Then the family started to arrive for Sunday lunch (and with seven children and all their offspring that is quite a lot of family) and she leapt to her feet and trotted off to greet them and I started the difficult task of extricating myself from Andalusian hospitality.

"Well, have a rosco I just baked (delicious almond pastry, light as a feather) at least."

"More coffee."

"Take a beer with you."

"Don't go yet, have a little glass of wine."

"Come back this afternoon."

In the end I was allowed to leave but not before promising to return for breakfast next day. No wonder Manolo is a little on the portly side, all that food and all that loving care.

I went and stood by the bank/"posada" with "Two Middle Aged Ladies in Andalusia" in my hand and read again all the little adventures that Penelope mentions there. She stayed four days in "Don Diego", and I think felt very at home here in spite of the "posada" being one of the draughtiest she had experienced. She mentions going to bed with her pyjamas over her underwear and her clothes over her pyjamas as the bitter wind blew in through the glassless windows. On her first night, she took a bottle of wine to bed with her to help her sleep as she says she was sleeping badly due to "over excitement". Just as she was getting pleasantly drowsy, two Guardia Civiles burst into her bedroom and demanded hers and the Marquesa's papers. This happened more than once when she was staying in "posadas" and I suppose there must have been a fair bit of horse-stealing in those days, with all the movement of livestock that went on throughout Andalusia. They were certainly more interested in the mare's papers than Penelope's and asked a lot of questions, guns slung over their shoulders and smoking cigarettes in her bedroom. Then they found her prayer book on the windowsill and, with a couple of "muy bien"s (very well's), left her in peace. Since the terrible plague of African Horse Flu caused the deaths and necessary euthanasia of so many equines throughout Spain in the 1980's, there are now very strict controls on all movement of horses on the peninsula and every single horse is microchipped, with huge fines if you omit to do this with your young stock. Of course everyone complains at all the bureaucracy involved but I think it is an excellent system and safeguards the legacy of the wonderful Spanish horses.

Next, a gloriously noisy lunch in one of the bars. There was football on TV full-blast, six tables of domino matches (Clack, clack , BANG!), several knife-edge card games (loud arguments and shouts of triumph) and constant tournaments of table football.

In the afternoon a watery sun peeped through and I met up with Manolo again and went down to his peaceful "finca" on the banks of the Rio Fardes. Curro, a huge mastin dog, soppy as a lover, greeted us, and a younger bitch rolled on her back to be tickled. Multi-coloured cats were sunning themselves on a row of horse carriages which was so unexpected in this virtually horse-free land I couldn't believe my eyes. In the stables were five fat glossy equines and he fed them, gently, lovingly and with no rush, and then the dogs and finally the soft mewing of the cats became a background of rolling purrs as they got their biscuit. I could tell he was enjoying himself. Manolo is one of the few people left in this area who is still involved with and passionate about horses. He told me how sad he is that only one of his seven children takes an interest and how very few people he knows with whom he can "talk horse". The gypsies are his horsey friends and they still get together to chat and compare animals. He used to have ten horses and he sowed the fields and fed them from the harvest, just as Rosendo, Penelope´s landlord, did for his mule; but then there were bad years and he started buying grain and now the fields are planted with olives.

He confirmed something I had already begun to suspect; many of the people of what are now the olive groves have taken against farm animals in a strange way, as if they represent the poverty and hunger of the old days. He told me how, when he hitches up his driving pair during the Feria, there are people who make a jeer of him and his passion. Unbelievably, the four carriages, both two and four wheelers parked in his barn, were made by Manolo and his older son.

"Through trial and error really. That first one turned out to be far too heavy so then we made the second lighter and so on. Trying to improve on each one. The harnesses I made too, and the mule packs using esparto grass. It is what I love to do"

It is indeed all a labour of love against the odds by one of the few remaining horsemen in these parts. I was really moved to think that someone who is just continuing what was once an integral part of the life here could, in such a relatively short time, be considered a lonely oddity.

There is a great tradition in Granada and Jaen provinces of a "tapa", often quite a large one, being provided with every drink. You do not choose your tapa, it is brought to you by the barman and they are often very original. This evening I had artichoke hearts with anchovy with the first glass, followed by cured cheese and some little white grapes, then real crackling - which my Irish teeth and I just didn't dare risk – and so on. This is an excellent method of having a cheap supper, though I was slow on the uptake thinking if I didn't order an alcoholic drink, I wouldn't warrant the tapa. In fact this is not the case and you get a tapa with a lemonade or a Coke. Luckily it turned out to be stocious Sunday for everyone else in the pub too with handsome young blokes all presuming I WAS Penelope and I began to think they might be right after knocking back all the drinks I ordered to make sure I got enough tapas.

Ah well, at least I didn't need to take a bottle of wine to bed to ensure my slumber and if the Guardia Civil did turn up I certainly never heard them.

April 8th

An idea in the garden of paradise

This morning was the village market day in Villanueva, so I went to investigate, knowing how faithfully Penelope described the food available fifty-eight years ago. The stalls were laid out in the streets around the square and there was plenty of fruit and vegetables on sale which would not have been such a necessary addition in the "Don Diego" days when everyone grew their own. The clothes on display were mainly working gear: strong trousers, rubber boots, overalls and thick socks, sturdy shoes and boots and protective gloves. There were also barrels of pulses, a mainstay of country cuisine, once considered the poor man's meat, soaked overnight and then used in salads or soups, stews and regional dishes, anything that made a little meat or fish go further. They would have been cooked in the "pucheros" and "cocidos" that Penelope describes sharing on those cold November days. The ladies of the village were buying pulses by the kilo, served out of their barrels in rattling red and white and brown and green scoopfuls - kidney beans, butter beans, lima beans, chickpeas, lentils and others I didn't recognise. The stall slap in front of the town hall was a huge colourful table of sweeties, a rainbow of chewable, suckable delights for everyone under twelve with the strong white teeth the Spanish kids all seem to be blessed with. Penelope would have had a field day, filling her pockets as she did in every village she passed through, trying to bribe her persistent "court" of children to leave her in peace.

I went to breakfast with Manolo, Carmela and Doña Encarna as promised, a spread of coffee, toast, tomato, oil and garlic, my staple at home – but with extras. There were Carmela´s homemade "roscos", honey from a neighbour´s hives and crumbly cured ham. Talk was of the theft of a cement mixer from their garden shed (a cave), but it seemed that there was history here and they knew who it was. Villages!

I decided to ride along the Rio Fardes valley a little way and explore. Penelope also rode this way during her stay in the village. She went bareback on account of the Marquesa´s girth gall which meant her attempts to mount after getting off to persuade the mare across a tricky bridge caused huge hilarity in some boys who were watching, until a kindly muleteer gave her a leg up. My handicap was having to take both horses as they had by now become so inseparable I feared that whichever one I left behind would cause a ruckus and possibly break through a fence. Normally I would never allow such hysterical nonsense but these circumstances, I felt, excused Luqa and Bruma. Riding on, day after day, through totally strange country, never returning anywhere, always striking out into the unknown, they had become each other´s home, each other´s familiar place and safety. I noticed how, when something potentially scary turned up along our way, they kept on striding out but shifted a little closer together, so their sides were touching – and, if it was really threatening, my leg was thoroughly squashed. So I excused them their interdependency.

The valley at the bottom of the wonderful gorge is known as the "vega". Not more than a few hundred meters wide, it is a fertile ribbon between the vast smooth vegetation-less hills of beige and cream and silver-grey. We followed a soft sandy trail that crossed the little river which rushed noisily along, full of its own importance. The Fardes runs southwest to northeast, nurturing what Penelope called a "garden of paradise" along its unassuming way. I wondered if this little watercourse is solely responsible for cutting down and down through the yielding rock to form such an extraordinary gash in the earth. Further downstream it joins the Guadiana Menor which subsequently flows into the great grand Rio Guadalquivir, cradle of dreams, of songs and civilisation, so maybe the little Fardes knows this in its heart and is rightly proud and confident.

Turning upstream among almond, peach and pomegranate trees the birdsong was deafening. The birds fluttered close to us and hopped from branch to branch, relatively unafraid, making it clear that I was the interloper in their territory, so I was able to get a good look at them. The hoopoes were there, of course, their "hoos" making a soft echoing background to the other songs and chirps and chatter. Some of the noisiest were Sardinian warblers, with a shock of black feathers on their little heads and perky red eyes. There were other warblers as well which I looked up later and, I think, were Bonelli's and Rufus, their clear piping notes piercing the air, and goldfinches galore with their continuous glittering song. Probably the most spectacular were the bee eaters, trilling and flashing their turquoise, orange and yellow livery from the tops of the tallest trees, hundreds of them. I hoped the bees who made my breakfast honey were not on their menu.

I rode Luqa and let Bruma loose to follow along behind. As the rock wall on the far side started to loom closer to the water, Luqa and I had to cross back and forth over the stream, dropping down the steep banks and jumping up the other side. Bruma, the drama queen, full of her flirtation with Paco's stallion, was meanwhile taking Becher's Brook leaps back and forth over the water and sometimes staying on the wrong side and tearing in mock panic through the orchards, tail in the air, mane flowing and blowing, scattering goldfinches and quince blossom. Luqa and I just rolled our eyes and left her to it until the stream flowed under a huge black precipice and we were forced, as was Penelope, to climb up onto the country road which runs from Villanueva to Guadix. I had a lunch date so we turned back towards the village and as we approached, we passed the cave house where Caridad had lived. It was quite recognisable from the photo in Penelope's book, though somewhat tarted up with railings and an entrance gate and nowhere obvious to tie your mule. Sixty years ago, as she sat and sewed or prepared the vegetables at the door of her cave, Caridad would have had exactly the same view from this higher ground, looking out across the grey green vega to the naked hills beyond, and it was this doorway that framed the lovely photo of the three boys playing dominoes against the light.

Paco, my horses' host, and his lovely happy wife Julia, cooked me a delicious "arroz caldoso" which is like a seafood paella with lots of broth. It seems a fishmonger comes in his van daily from Almeria so, although landlocked, the good folk of Villanueva de las Torres get plenty of the fruit of the sea.

Cuqui was very much in attendance following us between the stables and the house and trying to get my horses to join in her games.

Paco lives in a structural house of which there are now many in Villanueva. In 1961 there were only three streets of houses that were not dug out of the hillsides but I felt it might be a slightly snobbish thing in this day and age to not live in a cave; though with a constant temperature of 20° summer and winter and rock-solid foundations and walls (literally), most people I talked to seemed very pro the old ways. Behind their house the hill was filled with dwellings so after lunch we went, with Julia's garrulous and undaunted mother, to see inside some of the traditional houses. The first they took me to was beautifully restored and painted, full of genuine old furniture and artefacts. It was enormous, going back into the depths of the mountain with two fireplaces and pleasantly warm inside on this damp day. There were no inner doors, just traditional curtains made in the province of Granada, "Alpujarreñas", thus the air circulates and the front door is left open all day long so the atmosphere does not get stale. These curtains hang in front of all the village doors in Granada Province lest, as they say, "the sun eats the wood". In the cave houses the chimneys also act as air vents.

Next we saw a cave dwelling exactly as it would have been sixty years ago. There was a living room at the front with a huge chimney which housed a veritable cauldron for cooking suspended above the fire and, beyond, four bedrooms from whose rafters hung hams and sausages, peppers and garlic. Further back there was a large stable with space for two or three beasts, the manger carved out of the rock and a hay store beside it, the hay delivered through a hole in the mountain above! There was even a little enclosure for the hens. Everywhere there were niches and shelves carved in the walls for storage, and personal belongings. I thought how handy it would be to get your untidy teenager to just chip into the rock a bit deeper to make room for all their junk! It was extraordinary how safe, dry and comfortable it all felt. The one drawback in the old days would have been lack of light and the necessity of smoky olive-oil lamps but now they all have electricity. Unfortunately the positioning of the main pylon that brings it to that part of the village is a bit of a shame, blocking as it does the view from one of the highest and most glamorous dwellings. However, when I mentioned it, nobody seemed to have even thought about the aesthetics; they have light after all.

Emerging into the weak evening sunshine I saw in every direction hills and views and cave entrances that were the backdrop of Penelope´s photos and really felt she and La Marquesa might ride round the corner at any moment.

I was leaving next morning so I started the now familiar routine of walking some of my stuff from my room to the horses in advance. Then set about a certain amount of frantic "mucking out" of my quarters, trying to see it through the eyes of an impeccably-minded Spanish woman. Straw, mud, horsehair and even a few leaves from my ride in the vega seemed to have spread themselves throughout the little room and I thought how much easier it would be to get away with it all in a cave house, rather than the shiny-tiled interior favoured by the modern Spanish housewife. I went to see Doña Enriqueta to thank her and pay her and she seemed to have softened towards me now I hadn´t actually stabled the horses in my bedroom, asking about my plans and even whether I would be back!

Supper was an impromptu affair with Pepe Vallejo, Mayor of Villanueva de las Torres, and his brother Tomas both married to daughters of Juan Valle Martinez who had talked to me about Rosendo and Carmen yesterday morning. Two brothers marrying two sisters crops up quite a lot in Andalusian villages, making the children double-first cousins and furthering the close family links that hold these communities so firmly in place. We laughed a lot, especially as pretty well everyone in the room had now read my translation of the part of Two Middle-Aged Ladies pertaining to "Don Diego". Being of a younger generation, they thought Penelope's remarks about the interior of the posada, the general lack of privacy and the way the children reported on her every move, hilarious. Pepe has three children. One son is a Guardia Civil and the other is trained as a nurse and studying environmental health. His daughter is a food technician and works for a big canning and bottling company. Yes, of course, he confirmed, girls are expected to have a job now and not stay at home like the older generation of women did.

I asked him the question that had been bugging me. Why Barcelona? Why had so many of the people I enquired about in this village gone to Barcelona?

"Barcelona has always been somewhere with lots of work options. Here there was always agricultural work which meant you were never hungry but never had any money so we went there looking for something different. I went in '69 as a young lad and I remember on every door of building sites, mechanics, garages and shops there were notices saying 'workers wanted'. I stayed until 1975 then went to do the 'mili' (military service) and returned here but to this day, in spite of all the hoohaa we have up there at the moment [embarrassed grin as he is referring to recent activity by the Catalan Independence group] it is still a place of work and opportunity."

Conversation moved on to the big hope for the rejuvenation of Villanueva through Rural Tourism.

"Our treasure is the "Cuenca", the basin of the Rio Fardes and the amazing geological environment in which we live. This was all once an enormous lake, you know. We are working with thirty other villages on a project of a Geoparque (geological park). Unesco is interested - but it is complicated." (I should think so, with thirty other villages involved.) "Now we are fighting an intensive pig farm that one of the big companies wants to situate in our valley. Think of the effluent pouring into the Rio Fardes we cannot let it happen."

Please God NOOOO!

"First we have to educate the people who live here to become aware of what we have. We are working to identify walking routes in the Colorados, the beautiful mountains you will ride through tomorrow, and there is also a project to prepare empty cave houses for tourists to stay in. It is slow trying to get help and grants but we have something so special here."

Indeed they do, and it was while I was sitting round their table eating fruit from the vega of Villanueva de las Torres, once "Don Diego", that the beginnings of an idea crept into my head.

Spain is full of official walking routes, from the Gran Ruta 7 which purportedly goes from Tarifa to Athens, the Gran Senda de Malaga, three hundred kilometres around Malaga Province, and the well-known Camino de Santiago to the more humble local footpaths signed for walkers' use. What about bringing walkers and mountain bikers through the villages I was riding through? Villages that had no apparent tourism at all, rural or otherwise. Bring people in to eat at the bars, buy at the shops and sleep in "casas rurales" or caves. I know the ways and the paths; I have all the maps on paper or in my head, what about making it official - La Ruta de Penelope?

Of course the potential for dirt might finish off Doña Enriqueta.

Clockwise fromt top left: Doña Encarna , PC´s photo of Caridad at the door of her cave house with her family, some of her "court" of following children in Don Diego

*

April 9th

Mad dogs and crazy weather

I was up at dawn, but then I usually am. Some inbuilt mechanism makes me feel I must leap out of bed as soon as I wake or the good will go out of the day. Very tiresome for more relaxed friends and family. However, the sun was shining, the horses were waiting and we were ready for more adventures.

Manolo and Paco, the lone horsemen of Villanueva de las Torres, watched me tack up and load the pack saddle. Left alone, I now had feeding the horses and total preparation down to one hour but with conversation and constant questions I tended to slow down and get distracted – unlike most women I am not a multi-tasker. I mounted up and said my farewells and they waved us off a little wistfully. Bruma and Lucero the stallion's farewells lasted longer, echoing back and forth through the streets. We clattered along to have our picture taken with Mayor Pepe Vallejo in front of the Town Hall, flags hanging still in the golden early morning. (Turns out he was terrified of horses and Bruma shouting for her lover made him jump out of his skin!) As we rode out, Doña Enriqueta, in a newly-pressed pinny, was on her balcony to wave goodbye. I may have won her round. I briefly wondered if she had inspected my room yet: I had done my best, but I feared my best would not be hers. Who cared as we dropped down to the inviting trail beside the Rio Fardes, this time heading downstream?

On this day's route, Penelope had arranged for her landlady's first cousin, Juan *"…to guide me out of the infernal regions as there were no roads leading to my next port of call: only a labyrinth of mule tracks…over the pale grey sierras on the far side of the canyon. When Juan had first called at the posada two days earlier to fix terms, he wore his working clothes and had three days growth of beard on his chin. So I simply did not recognise him…He wore a neat blue suit and a grey homburg hat and had evidently just emerged from the barber's"*

I did not have a guide in a homburg hat on a sturdy pony to take me out of the enchanted valley, but I had traced on Wikiloc what I could ascertain from Penelope's description of the route, and my phone was in my pocket, waiting to pounce if I got it wrong. I reckoned the distance I needed to ride today was about thirty-eight kilometres. If I hadn't had my four legged cross country vehicles it would have been eighty-two by road.

Our sheltered way took us into the green "vega" alongside the bustling little river, through almond and olive groves, sugar cane and oleander. Every so often we came across concrete irrigation canals that forced us away from the water but we always found our way back. When the branches got lower and our path narrower, I decided to climb up to a higher track that served some of the farms in the valley. As we emerged from the "vega" a jeep raced down to us, a young man leapt out, grasped my hand in both of his and said,

"Penelope, I heard you were here. I am so pleased to see you again. What courage, what a wonderful journey you are on!"

It was all too surreal for me. I just smiled, shook his hand and wondered which of us was the ghost.

He directed me back down off the track, past groves of poplars standing ankle deep in water that reflected the azure skies above. We trotted on and on beside silver grey trunks, hazy and elegant, crowned by shimmering green leaves far above. Poplars are a fast growing crop used for making paper, a new idea since Penelope's time and a very beautiful addition. They are like sunlit cathedrals lit by the stained-glass windows of their emerald crowns in spring and golden shafts through their autumn foliage later in the year, and always the faint rustle, rustle from high above.

Eventually Wikiloc chirruped at our turn-off through a ruined farm whose name I had forgotten. Last night at supper, there had been talk of the starving dogs kept by an unscrupulous shepherd here to rent to hunters. Seprona, the animal cruelty prevention body, had been informed but had not yet come to deal with it. Thinking of the poor starving dogs, and in typical eejity foreigner style, I had filled my pockets with scraps and leftovers when no one was looking so I would have some offerings when I rode past. As we entered between the buildings some skeletal shapes peered out at us and I started to distribute alms. Suddenly we were totally surrounded by a ravenous, baying pack of what looked, to me, in my panic, like wolves, so thin they were almost transparent. They started to grab at my horses' legs and, dropping Bruma's lead rope, Luqa and I fled at the gallop. Bruma, well able to mind herself, lashed out in every direction, and when I looked over my shoulder, I even saw her going for some of the hounds with her teeth, ears flat back. Then she charged up alongside and for a long couple of minutes it was a dogs versus horses race. Eventually we drew clear and after another kilometre or so I dared to steady the horses back to a walk. By some miracle Bruma's pack was intact, which was just as well because I wasn't going back to retrieve anything. I was not surprised the prevention of cruelty people had not yet dealt with that lot.

Next we came to an "aldea" called, of course, Cortijo Nuevo or New Farm. When Pepe Vallejo lived here as a child it held one thousand people. Now it holds…..one guy. But a good guy I am sure because he had a big herd of goats which, being the first I had seen on my travels, were a very welcome sight. The rest of the place looked like something out of a Western movie - the deserted desert town where the bad guys are waiting. Old tarpaulins flapping in the wind, broken metal structures rattling, landslides of rock tumbling into the dirt lane and always the great grey hills. It would have been seriously spooky if it hadn't been for good goat guy who waved and smiled from his perch above it all among his merry skipping companions.

When we reached the farthest end of the gorge, the hills cuddled up around us, showing off their russet, ochre and scarlet hues. We found a bridge over the river where Penelope had had to hitch her legs up across the mare's shoulders to avoid getting wet, and then we started the spectacular climb up out of "the inferno". Penelope was as moved by the landscape as I was.

"We then rode along a soft grey track that led up into the bare

beautifully modelled clay hills of Giotto's frescoes. As we got higher there was an even wider view of the river valley below and the interminable grey sierras beyond it. This sort of landscape gives you an insight into Eternity: it is so vast and beautiful and so still that you would like it to go on forever."

The wide trail zigzagged up and up and up. I sympathised with Bruma whose curiosity caused her to stop and gaze back the way we had come and then jog a bit and stop again to look, but I was mounted on Luqa of the long swinging stride and "let's get on and reach the top" mentality, so once again I let the little mare make her own way up. As we powered off in front of her, catch ups started to involve rather a lot of celebratory bounds and handstands and she began to dislodge the pack, which was not secured to my usual standards due to the spectators when I was doing it earlier that morning. On a high, exposed hairpin bend, about two hundred metres above the valley, I had to get off and repack everything. The views below were magical, the river a tiny silver ribbon curling among the poplars which resembled asparagus beds from up here. To the south the velvety hills looked as if they were covered with crumpled bedsheets that some giant had tossed aside as he rose.

We continued to climb and I planned a break and a picnic when we crested the top but up there it was a completely different climate. Rain, on a strong wind, slapped us in the face as we reached the end of our three-hundred metre climb and, ahead of us on the high plain, trees were bending to the weather and clouds scudding black and ominous. Heads down, we rode straight into the downpour, no thought of pausing for a picnic now.

Off to our right lay Cuevas del Campo where Penelope

and her guide had called in for lunch, but we were taking the fastest direct line to our next stop, the squall bouncing off the now metalled road that took us across the exposed altiplano. As we slithered along a cycle track, trucks and cars appearing and disappearing in a sizzle of wet tyres and a flash of headlights, someone phoned me from far away Ronda to tell me he had found a horse, saddled with no rider, and could I come and see if I recognised it! Explain as I might, dear José Maria simply could not take on board where I was or what I was doing and, clutching my phone in a sodden hand, I seemed unable to politely finish the call! Just a reminder that other people have lives too.

If I had been faithful to the two middle-aged ladies I would have stopped in Pozo Alcon, a relatively big and busy town where they spent the night (and made rude remarks about the drains). However, I had done my best to contact the Town Hall there to enquire about horse accommodation and no one had ever replied. Surfing the area online, I found the amazing words "Equestrian Centre" in nearby Hinojares and immediately got in touch with José Coronado, the delightful owner, who said, absolutely and of course there was room for the horses and incidentally they had a little hotel where I could stay. Job done.

I say "nearby" Hinojares but that wet day on the blasted heath, it didn´t seem near at all. As we plod, plod, plodded on I became very aware that I had not covered the pack with the tarp I had for that purpose and all my own waterproofs were buried somewhere out of reach. By the time we dropped down to the deep basin where the little village of Hinojares hides, we were in a sorry state of shivering misery but José was waiting and helped me unload the drenched pack, tack and sheepskin into a dry tack room and stable the horses among all of his. Lots of new friends for them to talk to. Then he took me to the most cosy, comfortable little hotel I had stayed in so far. My God, there was heating and a bath and a TELLY!

These luxuries are now commonplace in Andalusia but unheard of in 1961.

Penelope Valentine Hester Chetwode, being one of the "gentry", would have been brought up in comfortable circumstances but, rather typically of the intrepid British women of her class, did not flinch if she had to rough it. She was born in the cavalry barracks in Aldershot, England on February 14th 1910. Her father, Philip Chetwode, was a soldier, a cavalryman, who later became Commander-in-Chief of the British Army in India. Brought up in the usual manner of aristocratic young ladies of the era, in private schools and being "finished" in France and Italy, she inherited her father´s undying passion for horses, ridden and driven and her mother, Star´s, delight in exploration on horseback. She was a reluctant debutante but learnt Art History in Italy and this became her second passion. She also picked up the Italian language much more quickly than her peers so had an ear for languages which must have helped her with her Spanish, non-existent when she came to Spain, but progressing speedily during her month-long ride. Aged eighteen, to avoid the amorous advances of a young man her mother thought unsuitable, she was shipped off to India where she fell in love again, this time with the country and all things Indian.

In 1933 she married Poet Laureate-to-be John Betjeman, and they settled down in the remote Berkshire Downs, near the ancient White Horse of Uffington, cut into the chalk hillside millennia ago. They had two children Paul and Candida, later Candida Lycett-Green, also a writer, and Penelope continued to ride and drive a variety of horses and traps around the countryside.

In 1961, when she came to Spain, her children, born at the beginning of the Second World War, would have been in their early twenties, and husband John seemed to be spending a lot more time in London or travelling than in whichever little country house she was hoping he would return to. In fact she does mention at one point on her Spanish odyssey that he had written to her from Australia. Her conversion to Roman Catholicism in 1948 may have distanced her from John who was a staunch Anglican, known for his much-loved poems about the rituals and buildings of the Church of England. Her devotion to her new faith is very obvious in her writing and she never missed an opportunity to attend mass. Of course, in those days, the parish priest was the best source of information and contacts in the villages she passed through. Rather as I asked the mayor of each place to help and advise me, the priest was often the first person she went to after she had settled La Marquesa in the posada. Towards the end of her trip she even managed to have quite deep theological discussions with the local "parroco" (parish priest) which shows that her Spanish must have improved by leaps and bounds.

Penelope Chetwode Betjeman's energy, enthusiasm and sense of humour, combined with a natural command, if you like bossiness, typical of the British upper classes of that time, went down well in Andalusia where the women in particular have a naturally high self-esteem and conviction that they are right! You only have to see an Andalusian woman, no matter what age, shape or looks, rise to dance Flamenco and make the room her own, knowing she is beautiful, desirable and powerful. Penelope certainly met her match with the hundreds of children who followed in her wake in the remote villages of Granada and Jaen Provinces and completely failed to be subdued by her ultimatums to leave her in peace. Yet her interest and kindness among these people who were so far from what she would have considered her normal way of life, shines through in every word she writes about them.

I was the only person in the hotel so José, and his jolly sister Pilar, asked me to go along to the local bar to join them and friends from Alicante for supper. Carmela and Pepe and their son and his boyfriend had been staying in a cave house rented from José and this was their last night. They visit often and were in fact taking five Bodeguero pups back home from José's stables for themselves and friends in Alicante. This breed descends from the Jack Russell terriers brought over originally by the British who were involved in the Jerez wine business (sherry). The little ratters were used to keep the wine cellars or "bodegas" free of vermin and so became known as Bodegueros.

It was a very merry evening, partly because the guy who ran the bar recognised me from a recce I had made earlier in the year and apologised that he had no Jameson. So I had to show I didn't mind and have far too much JB instead. I was among people who had travelled but returned to their roots: for example Pilar, known as Pili, had spent nine years living in Switzerland before returning to Spain, and there was a certain sophistication in the group sitting round the table which I had not yet found on my journey.

Fully aware that I was being somewhat unfaithful to La Ruta de Penelope, in the wrong village, in much too luxurious a setting when she had slept in the bitterly cold posada in Pozo Alcon, I snuggled unrepentantly into my gloriously comfortable bed and thought of the horses, cosy in their dry stables as the rain continued to beat down.

*

April 10th

When muleteering and hospitality are in the blood

When I was planning this ride I factored in non-riding days to allow me time to do detective work as necessary regarding the two middle-aged ladies who had passed this way so long ago. I had also taken account of a couple of feed deliveries coming in friends' cars to be dropped ahead on my trail, no horse feed being available locally any more. When kind friends were prepared to do the four or five-hour drive to bring the horse feed, the least I could do was stop my own little adventure for a day or two to keep them company. Yet the daily rhythm of preparing, packing, mounting up and moving on was so exciting, elating and in a strange way soothing, I was becoming addicted and found my stops seemed longer and less welcome than I had expected. Of course Penelope had no such need to plan, she just rode gaily along (yes, she would have used that word) in the general direction of villages that appeared on her hopelessly inaccurate map and saw what the day brought forth. As I was trying to follow in her hoof prints, I could not be so freewheeling about where I ended up each night.

However, this morning the rest was very welcome. I felt

more than middle-aged as I was still in recovery from yesterday. All the old injuries were complaining like mad from being so cold and wet, and there are plenty of those from a lifetime with horses. Not that my childhood riding and hunting in Ireland and later life working with international polo teams involved many crashing falls. I have been lucky and never broken a bone from falling off. (I have never said or written that down before so will add a "so far" and grasp a bit of wood.) I have the remnants of random incidents like a stallion bite on my arm which is still blue thirty years on, several broken toes from being jumped on, a smashed and repaired elbow from a polo ball and a confused bit of vertebra from an iron bar that came away when a horse pulled back on one of the tours I was running in the Serrania de Ronda. In fact it is the legacy of the kick of a cow that hit me square on my chubby little thigh and threw me across the milking parlour leaving a permanent indent when I was eight that is probably the worst of all! Everything has miraculously healed and is no trouble in day-to-day life but they rear their nasty little heads when chilly, damp and long hours in the saddle kick in. I realised today that I had a new injury to haunt me: chorizo finger woke up with an ugly throb, having been fairly quiescent lately. I had taken to flinging myself into the arms of the lovely friends and endless cousins I was introduced to and kissing them firmly on both cheeks rather than risk a handshake.

I found the horses happy as pigs in shite, a long line of neighbours in the stables and a couple of hours in the top paddock to themselves so they could roll and revel in the mud. Bruma had a bit of a rub from wet paniers which might explain her stopping dead from time to time as we rode the last endless strait into the rain yesterday, so I was glad to be able to rest them. While I was there Carmela and Pepe and the boys trooped in to pick up the five little Bodeguero pups and take them to their new homes in Alicante. Terrier mum heaved a sigh of relief as they were driven away and stretched out her poor sore pink bottles to the emerging sunshine.

It was hard to find a time when José Coronado and his sister Pilar could talk to me. They are not obviously brother and sister. José, in his mid-forties, is tall and dark and Pili a few years older, smaller and comfortably round and smiley. I managed to pin them down in the hotel sitting room today before more guests started arriving for the weekend. They told me how their grandfather's family were merchants, buying and selling mules to take to the market in Guadix. They also drove sheep and lambs to Baza where there was another market for buying, selling and exchanging animals, the traders coming by the same route I had ridden yesterday and also from the west. The old drove roads, "cordeles", lead from central Spain all the way to the coast, known as direction "Levante". This same route was used by the original Iberians thousands of years ago. José and Pili's grandfather and uncle stopped the trading tradition in the 1970's when the bottom fell out of the market for mules and emigration had eaten into the population of the area, though their father continued trading lambs to Baza.

José, the youngest of three children, trained as a PE teacher, mainly so he could stay in his village and the mountains he loves. He took children to summer camps in the Parque Natural de las Sierras de Cazorla, Segura y Las Villas, henceforward to be known as Cazorla Natural Park because that really is a bit of a mouthful! Hinojares lies just within the boundaries of the park and there José met a Forest Ranger who offered him a job and in a few months they were talking about opening a Rural Tourism business. Due to emigration from these villages, there were plenty of locals with extra houses that could be made into rental properties for holidaymakers. They are known as "Casas Rurales" which means rural houses but in this case specifically for tourists. The two young men started to help them prepare and welcome tourists. However, there was a level of frustration, as José says, the local people really had no idea how to treat the outsiders and were reluctant to up their game to accommodate people looking for a little more than the basics.

"At first my friend and I would meet the guests when they arrived and make sure they had everything they needed and be on call for them. We have such fantastic natural resources here with the Natural Park on our doorstep, there were plenty of guests. After two or three years we tried for a bit more quality but none of the house owners were interested so we started with our own houses. I invested in "Casas Cuevas de Cazorla" ("Cazorla Cave houses") with my cousin Jose Ramon and we set up "Active Tourism" with hiking, canoeing and climbing in the mountains here. After another four years my father suggested horse riding. He helped me choose the horses and then he taught me to ride at the age of twenty-six! Can you believe it, a muleteer's son and I had never ridden? But I love it, I have it in the blood, I suppose. Everybody said I was complicating my life and of course I was, but a good complication."

José's cave houses, which seem to be doing a roaring trade, are beautifully presented with such details as jacuzzis, open fires, barbecues and even a little swimming pool with a stunning view, and he meets all the guests personally.

Ever the entrepreneur, José showed me a photo of a "salina" or salt pan he has bought with a grand old house still standing beside it.

"I have bought it with another cousin and we want to see if we can regenerate the tradition. The Romans gathered here because there was salt, and of course paid the "salary" of the workers with it. There were two "Salinas", both producing until the 1960's. That house was abandoned only eight or nine years ago. It is an 18th century manor house and the bell tower has only just fallen down We want to restore it and start producing salt again. The spring that gives the salt is still functioning and it is very good quality."

José and Pili's grandmother on the other side of the family was from a long line of posada owners so it does seem that Pili, who was living in Madrid with her husband and two sons when José proposed the hotel idea to her, was bound to come back. Once again it must have been in the blood.

"We came back with two teenagers and it wasn't easy but our mother's mother ran the posada here in the village and her name was also Pilar so it was meant to be. My husband cooks and I do all the bookings and so on and we have been here thirteen years now. Life is a sequence, you know. José is back on our grandfather's trails with the animals and I am welcoming people passing through to our hostelry like our grandmother."

In 1961, when Penelope was in Pozo Alcon, she met an engineer working on the dam for the La Bolera reservoir in the mountains to the north and his dis-satisfied wife who was from Madrid and not pleased to be holed up in a one-mule town because of her husband's work. Penelope, practical as ever, suggested she bought a horse and explored the countryside and was quite surprised when the lady in question did not seem to think this a good idea. I am sure the gently brought up "Madrileña" had no intention of taking advice from this crazy foreign woman, travelling alone and braving the terrors of bandits and who-knew-what-other dangers in the wilderness. The dam was specifically for watering the huge amount of cereal crops that used to grow on the plain I had crossed yesterday which, long before man came to cultivate it, had been part of an enormous inland sea. The olives that existed then were just planted at the edge of the fields, enough for each household to have oil for the coming year. In José and Pili's grandparents' time, there was work for everyone, scything by hand from dawn to sunset all summer long. As well as the salt pans, there were flour mills and olive mills and a green glass factory, all in Hinojares. Some of the huge green wine containers, "damajuanas" (Lady Janes) can still be found in local houses. When the olives arrived en masse, the reservoir to water them all was right there.

In the afternoon, José very kindly took me in his jeep, with his helper at the stables, Francis, in the back seat, to see if I thought the paths I would take out of Hinojares on Saturday would be accessible for a pack pony. He was also trying to ascertain how on earth Francis, known as Fran, had got so lost a few days ago leading a group of riders. I totally sympathised with José, having had many wonderful volunteers helping with my week-long treks through the mountains of Andalusia and I was always astonished to find some of the most hard-working and intelligent of them had no sense of direction at all. José's conversation with Fran was very familiar.

"So how did you end up here? …..But why did you turn

off there? ….No, you do that on the other trek on the other side of the mountain….You mean you came down that really steep bit? Dios mio! ….and then you turned LEFT? But why? …..didn't you recognise the dead tree/the lake/the village over there/?"

I read somewhere that your orientation mechanism is situated in a bit of the brain that is more or less developed WHEN YOU ARE BORN. So you pop out ready prepared either as an explorer and pathfinder or one of those who spend time trying to find their way out of the proverbial paper bag.

We drove along the valley of the Guadiana river – hello Rio Fardes, are you in there somewhere, do you remember me? – with strange white and pink rocks scooping and sweeping above and below us. We passed a craggy hilltop containing an Iberian settlement near Ceal, dating from 8000 BC and dropped down to yet another "aldea" in a fertile valley containing only twelve people now. It used to have many posadas to house the drovers using the old "cordel" which runs through it heading for the "Levante". Finally we walked the little path that José was worried about. It was fairly precipitous and the narrow zigzags with an occasional handrail made it complicated with a wide pack. I decided to pack Luqa on Saturday as he carries everything higher and can possibly avoid the lower narrows and squeeze himself and his pack between the rocks and banks. If the worst came to the worst, I could just unpack him before the most restricted corners and lug it through by hand, though there is nowhere to tie horses among the bare rocks and letting go of both at once always offers them the opportunity of fecking off without me.

I was delighted to see two flocks of sheep with attendant

dogs, goats and shepherd on our afternoon bouncing and ric-ocheting off tracks that would have been a lot more comfort-able and possibly safer on horseback. The animals have been looking plumper as we approach the more prosperous Sierra de Cazorla region and some of the dogs I saw today were al-most fat. The first flock was happily gorging down in the valley by the "aldea" but the second was up on the high tops in the care of Amador, impeccable in an embroidered waistcoat and smoking a cigar. Now that is definitely a first in my long career of scrutinising shepherds. Amador and José were friends and conversed for some time on the vagaries of a Town Hall that still had not repaired the deeply gullied trail that he needed to bring his car along to watch his livelihood. His flock was three hundred strong, half goats and half sheep grazing two well-separated hillsides, by their own choice, proof, as far as Amador was concerned, that every being on earth is naturally racist. I wished I had my phone or my camera with me to get a shot of this great character but I had come as unencumbered as possible to make a change from carrying my world in my pack saddle.

As we left I spotted a woman with a little blond boy in Amador´s car.

"Oh yes, that is his wife, she is a shepherdess too"

It started to pour with rain again in the evening and I felt a bit glum but went back for seconds of patatas bravas (spicy potatoes, in this case very spicy) which nearly blew my head off and counted my blessings – warm dry place for me, horses likewise.

From top: Climbing up out of the magical gorge, a rest stop on the way up, Marquesa the Second with Angela

April 11th

Chilblain posada and marquesa the second

I had intended to ride back to Pozo Alcon today to search for traces of Penelope but the horses were really enjoying their gossip and social diversions at José's stables and I remembered too clearly the dreary, samey trail back across the plain and it seemed pointless to put Mademoiselle and Himself through that again. Also, no one could suggest where I would safely leave them tied in the town when I arrived so, between the jigs and the reels, I decided to cheat and accept Pili's offer of a lift. She was going to town to have her hair done before her son and his thirteen friends (all medics from Malaga) arrived to spend the weekend at the hotel. In the car on the way there, I translated Penelope's description of her visit to have a wash, cut and set in the same town – water heated in the hairdresser's tiny front room so she could kneel on the floor, bowing her head *"as for decapitation"* in front of a chair with the seat removed and replaced by a basin of water. Both she and the hairdresser's little daughter, handing out the rollers as her hair was set, were frozen with the cold wind blowing in. She was charged 15 pesetas for the wash, cut and set and paid 25 as she felt it was far too little. Pili laughed a lot along the "how times have changed" vein and wished she could get a hairdo for 15 pesetas (€0.09).

Penelope stayed in the bitterly cold but grandly named Parador del Carmen. As well as taking overnight guests, folk could tie up their animals in the first part of the huge courtyard while their owners shopped or drank at the bar. For this they were charged a few cents. Further in was the stabling where La Marquesa was stowed, packed to bursting with all the dealers' and travellers' animals, probably including some of Jose and Pili's relations. Returning from church yet again, Penelope describes the scene,

"Back from evening devotions I went to the stable to give the Marquesa her supper but could not open the door for the sheep that were leaning against it. Eventually forced my way in and fell flat across a fat ewe. She smelt deliciously of lanoline. When I finally got to La Marquesa there was another ewe lying on the chopped straw in her manger. She looked so cosy that I could not bear to dislodge her, so I moved the mare down a peg. Beside the sheep there were several large pigs, a string of nine mules, five donkeys, seven goats, two ponies, two white turkeys and a lot of chickens in the stable which resembled Noah's Ark. As I left I caught the naughty Marquesa directing a sly kick at one of the pigs."

Perhaps because it would obviously have been tricky for such busy and crowded quarters to double as a ladies' and gentlemens' "convenience", the Parador del Carmen had the truly startling innovation of a loo on the landing. It wasn't perfect as the door would burst open of its own accord after thirty seconds and one of the panes of frosted glass was missing so anyone passing by could look right in on the unfortunate occupant. Due to snow on the nearby Sierra del Pozo, Penelope found this posada particularly chilly, with the north-facing window in her room also glassless, and missed her Dayella pyjamas that had fallen out of her saddle bags the day before as she galloped away from a bristly bandit on a donkey who demanded money from her on her way to Pozo Alcon. However, when she was wandering up the hilly streets in the evening light next day to take photographs, one of the young women sewing in her doorway called the tall Englishwoman in and presented her with her pyjamas. She explained that the donkey rider had picked them up on the trail and left them for her – so perhaps he wasn´t such a bandit after all!

I found the Parador del Carmen still standing, but bolted and barred. It is indeed an enormous house and right beside it is a little lottery shop where Yolanda, whose grandparents were the owners in 1961, works. I waited while this pretty girl listened to the pains of many who had come in to buy hope for a fresh start from her. She was so sympathetic and patient with everyone I was sure the hardworking family that once owned the posada must have been as kind as her. There were nine children that Penelope was introduced to and later they had a tenth. That baby was actually on the way when she was staying there. It took me a certain amount of digging to find one of the children who would remember Penelope. Yolanda, obviously the wrong generation, put me in touch with various uncles and aunts in both Pozo Alcon and Hinojares who all insisted I must talk to Maria Tiscar, the oldest sister. Where was she? Yup, in Barcelona!

So I phoned Maria, known as Mariquita by the family, and

she remembered plenty.

Maria Tiscar, fair haired and blue eyed, called after the lovely Virgin in the cave on the mountain, recalled Penelope very well.

"I can remember the moment she rode into town. I was thirteen and I can see her now, clearly. She was very elegant and pretty. Tall and strong. She looked so beautiful when she mounted up on that horse. For us this was something so new and extraordinary and I wished so much to be like her "

Maria Tiscar also confirmed there was a seventeen-year-old girl who helped out, another Maria, with flashing black eyes and dark hair who worked in the Posada at that time, flirting, as Penelope mentioned, with all the handsome young men who came to stay. (Among the guests were a pig dealer, various dam engineers, and a very charming and courteous mule trader who, Penelope reckoned if he discarded his smock for white tie and tails, would not have been out of place at the grandest dinner party. On reflection it seems this may well have been Jose and Pili's uncle.)

The children's father, the landlord, had spent his time trading almonds and ham between Alicante and Barcelona before he settled down and started making all those babies. When they opened the posada there was a much harsher climate than now in Pozo Alcon. Maria Tiscar remembers how much snow there used to be all and every winter and the really terrible chilblains some of the children suffered from. They were still filling the water tanks for the posada by hand with "cantaros" carried from the village wells and it would often freeze and the children's hands with it as they helped their father carry the containers every day.

"Oh my goodness, the pain of those chilblains. Mine used to swell so much they were purple and they used to bleed. Our father died young, aged forty-five, when I was about sixteen and after that I helped my mother and more or less ran the place. It was very hard work: the other children were still at school. We stopped taking in the animals around then but we still let people use the downstairs as a garage. I remember I charged them 1 peseta to leave a bicycle there and a bit more for a motorbike! When I was twenty, I married and came to Barcelona. I have two sons and a daughter and two of them have blue eyes like me and like my father. I go back every three years or so to visit the graves of my parents and our youngest brother, Juan Carlos, the tenth child who died in his thirties. But the town is very short of people now. In those days there used to be eight thousand, now it is down to about four thousand."

It certainly didn't feel short of people to me. By far the busiest place I had been in lately, the pavements were jostling with people and the streets hooting with cars. For the first time in Andalusia I was actually approached by a beggar (OK I don't get out much) when a swarthy woman with a sharp face came and stuck her upturned palm in my chest. I wondered if she was a descendant of the money-demanding, pyjama-returning donkey rider.

I went, of course, to inspect the church in Pozo Alcon and found it very changed since Penelope went to mass here. She would have gone to the Renaissance style church, founded in 1618 which, due to imminent collapse, was demolished in the mid-sixties and replaced. The present building was stark and modern enough to take my breath away. The ceiling however was rather splendid with beautiful wooden beams, the work,

111

Maria Tiscar told me, of one of her brothers-in-law who was a carpenter. The new church was unexpected and yet not out of context with the surrounding streets where ugly concrete blocks jostle the dear old gentle stately houses which look as if they may at any moment be pushed over.

I entered the building to find a meeting in progress about the Holy Week parades, a very important annual event in every village. There were three priests and a variety of hunky local boyos, the "costeleros" who carry the saints and holy figures on the measured, slow, solemn processions that go on long into the night of Holy Thursday and Good Friday. This job is much sought after and boys who scarcely ever darken a church's door will drive many miles for the honour of carrying the blessed figures on their "tronos" or thrones in another town if their own sacred icons are fully booked. Brotherhoods are linked to every blessed saint and, in Spain, where brotherhoods are involved, passions run high. In rows, on long tables at the end of the church, were the junior school's models of the various figures, each on their decorated float, each easily recognisable as one of the wooden or plaster statues in the church. These saints, the virgins of pain and of sorrows and the Christ figure carrying his heavy cross would have witnessed the tall foreigner with the wind-reddened face taking the sacrament in this place, but the modern stained-glass windows held no such link with the past.

I had been told to sit outside on the benches by the church as often older people gathered there who could chat to me about old times. So I sat in the sun for quite a while, while the "older people" took one look at this weird, old, foreign person and her odd outfit (most of my clothes were in the wash and I had borrowed from those a little larger than me) and changed their minds about sitting in their usual spot, scuttling by without meeting my eye. So I drew a blank there.

Luckily, Pozo Alcon was bursting with shops of all shapes and sizes so I was able to get a tiny gas canister for my tiny gas stove, some more protein sachets for when I really have no access to real food, and cider vinegar as a fly repellent for the horses. Then Pili turned up looking glamorous with new "roots", not of the genealogical variety, and we drove back to the peaceful streets of Hinojares.

I found José and his daughters, Maria and Angela aged sixteen and eight, at the stables making a pet of the latest arrival which everybody doted on. The union of José's Spanish stallion and his pretty bay mare, Chispa, had resulted in a dear little filly foal, born on April 1st, the day I set off on my adventure. Produce of a dappled silver father and a shiny terracotta mother, she looked for the moment as if she was going to turn out dun coloured, like Bruma, with a sandy little body, black legs and mane and tail. They announced that they had decided to call their little treasure "Marquesa" to mark my visit and expedition which touched me hugely and is one of the most exciting things that has happened on my journey so far.

April 12th

A merry dash around the mountain

Today took on a different hue with the arrival of two icons from my home town, Gaucin.

Diana Paget and Sally Von Meister are the epitome of the original British abroad tradition. With more than fifty years of living in Spain between them they are the very best sort of expats who remain staunchly British while becoming absorbed in the culture they have adopted, knowledgeable and enthusiastic about everything.

If you need to find out the best viewpoint for watching the hundreds of horses, mules, carriages and flamenca Señoritas crossing the Rio Guadalquivir on rafts during the Pilgrimage of the Rocio, they will direct you – and tell you the best bar to have seafood and "fino" while you watch. No hidden tapas establishment used only by the locals escapes their notice; if the top "rejoneadores" (bullfighters on horseback) are coming to the vicinity they know about it before the rest of the village. The most strategic balcony to watch the Semana Santa parades in Sevilla? No problem, Sally has the secret. The place they used to make those wonderful esparto birds? Diana can take you there. If I want to know which paths to take on my peregrinations in the Serrania de Ronda, I ask one of them. They will tell me, with additional stories of vodka-laced mad night-time rides when they lost six horseshoes on one stretch and the Spanish guide´s horse got colic because he hadn´t been out of a stable for a month but was quickly cured by putting a hose up his arse.

The Andalusians totally understand when they mince no words and call a spade a bloody shovel, while some of the more recently-arrived and urban ex-pats are a little stunned, if not shocked by these two feisty ladies. When I had my riding business I saw the disbelief on the more nervous riders´ terrified faces, as they tipped too far forward in the saddle and Diana advised them on their riding position,

"Sit so the farts come up the front, as my father would have said." Her father came second in the Grand National so who can argue with that?

Anno Domini has slowed them down a little (but that just means that the black runs in the ski resorts of Europe no longer see them every winter and their cars have replaced the horses), so now they avidly join in spirit with anyone who is adventuring out into the Spain they know so well. I was not at all surprised when they announced they knew the riding area I was going to, having made expeditions here twenty or so years ago and nor was it unexpected that they wanted to meet up and help. Who better to come with horse feed for my third week on the road?

So here they were, voices unmistakable, amazingly only

one small dog in attendance (I had been specific about this with visions of the flocks and herds of Granada and Jaen flying before the jaws of a pack that had just spent four hours in the car, little did I know then that there were hardly any flocks or herds). Their vehicle was packed to the gills with all the horse feed I had bagged up before my departure. They had also brought such things as they considered essential to my pilgrim's progress including a bottle of whiskey, Red Cell vitamins in case the horses needed a boost too, energy-filled nuts, more delicious snacks than I could eat in three weeks, a sack of carrots for the horses and a birthday cake for me! On top of all this we then had to stuff in the hay which I was buying from Jose, enough bales for a week. It took Jose, Fran and me five minutes of pushing to get the car door shut. That poor car. I am not sure to this day if Sally has managed to get all the hay off the ceiling!

So off we set, Bossy - small terrier, princess complex – horrified at the lack of space and bedding she was accustomed to in the back of the car - with Diana, shoehorned in, sitting on top of a mound of hay, feet on the carrots, birthday cake between her knees and unable to straighten her neck. I did try to make her sit in front but there is absolutely no point arguing with Diana Paget. The pleasant, gravelled road that Penelope rode north towards Cazorla is now tarmacked, slippery, curling and steep with crash barriers on both sides ensuring no horses could get out of the way if a big vehicle came hurtling down. Crash barriers are called "quita miedos" or "fear removers", and there are certainly a fair amount of spots on that climb into the mountains where it is quite nice to have your fears removed. After just over an hour we saw Cazorla ahead, nestled below sheer rock walls where various virgins, shrines and "ermitas", little chapels, clung above the town by their sacred fingernails.

*

I had come to recce Cazorla back in February, as I planned to hole up here during the Easter Week parades and it was essential I found somewhere safe for the horses. It is a fair-sized town and, because of its proximity to the enormous Natural Park that bears its name, fills up with tourists during the holidays. Elisa Mirangels, very successful restaurateur and my oldest friend in Spain, came with me and we concentrated on horse accommodation first. Walking around the outskirts and above the town we spent two days looking for little pockets of paddocks or olive groves that might house two very well-behaved and tired horses. Following the little Rio Cerezuelo along tortuous paths and then up and over ridges we circled the basin that Cazorla sits in, skirting under dramatic towers and forts and castles and talking to everyone we met. It was so beautiful up there, Cazorla in the warm sun, white crooked houses with honey-coloured roofs stretched at our feet and the little plazas and streets below bathed in the sunshine. But all to no avail. Sandwiched between the bare rock, every spare square metre of earth was crowded with vegetables or vines or fruit trees and no one could help us in our quest. On the third day, Elisa left and her parting shot, that I had better forget Cazorla for the horses, spurred me on! I strode through the squashed streets of the historic old town and into the huge marble halls of the "Ayuntamiento" or Town Hall where I knocked on doors, interrupted meetings, and talked to every single person I met crossing the hallowed ground (most of whom were seeking help as I was). It was all so much grander than I had been used to in the Town Halls of the little villages where everyone from the Mayor down was easily accessible, but I just hung around in the vast building all morning until it was suggested I talked to Nuria, the Cultural "Consejal" or councilor. She was, of course, in a meeting in a town thirty kilometres and I was definitely panicking so her secretary got her on the phone and she directed me downstairs to Martin, who is, I think, the "Youth" "Consejal". I explained yet again my project and what I was looking for and, after one minute to consider my request, he said

"Well, what is wrong with the bullring? We have no bull-fights at Easter, nothing until the Blues concert in July. They will be safe in there."

*

Now, with our loaded car, we drove into the town to pick up the key and leave four days' worth of horse feed in the bull-ring. I had been a little nervous of this arrangement because if I couldn't find anyone to give me a key all would be lost. I had made several phone calls and it seemed the people to go to were the "Policia Local". Cazorla was a seething mass of traffic and tourists, two days before Palm Sunday and things were heaving. Leaving Sally and Diana (still bent double in the back of the car) circling a very small and busy roundabout in one central square, I belted along a tiny street into the next plaza and sprinted to the police station. Closed. A phone number on the door. With shaking hands I rang it and an officer answered tersely saying the town was so busy they were all out on patrol. He knew about the key and I must come back in a few hours. Bizarrely I realised the voice arguing with him amid the cacophony of engines and horns coming down the phone was Sally's! She wanted to stay where she was because she was waiting for her "amiga"- friend. So I raced back along the crowded street, skipping in and out of a myriad of high heels and push chairs and families of eight who would not separate to let me through, went up to the poor policeman, who by this time was totally bemused, and told him I'd be back. Leaping in the car so we could stop holding up the traffic, I realised he probably hadn't even seen Diana in the back, disguised as she was among the hay, or there might have been a fine!

Next we drove around the mountain to the north where a road takes wheeled traffic into the Natural Park of Cazorla. It is a long way round and in a few days I hoped to drop directly down into the town from the high peaks with Bruma and Luqa. I had found out about someone who had horses deep in the forest near a campsite where I could stay which would be on my route so we were going to leave horse feed with him. We reached Cristobal's peaceful glade with corrals beside the infant Guadalquivir.

Diana, who has a tendency to shock and pretends she doesn't know she is, then started on one of her matchmaking projects. She is an incurable romantic and tends to decide who she considers likely to fall in love with whom and then – and this is the dangerous bit – she thinks they have! So off she went in both languages about how wonderful he would be for me, how lovely the place was and, when he showed us inside his cabin and she saw the double bed, why was I going to sleep in the campsite when I could be blissfully happy staying with him? I don't know quite how much Cristobal understood but he was the perfect gentleman and never showed any embarrassment. I, on the other hand, wanted to dump the horse feed, get in the back of the car among the remaining hay, and flee.

Back in Cazorla, the car parked this time, I once again jogged along to the Police Station, fingers and toes crossed. The police were all there but...they didn't have the key. More hanging around and I felt bad for the ladies waiting in the other plaza but I needn't have worried, they had got stuck into the vodka by then and were quite happy. At this point the police all left again, locking the station behind them and leaving me standing on the pavement. "Just wait here, don't move". Aagh! Eventually the "Jefe de Obras", or Project Manager, of the Town Hall turned up in a white van with a key he had cut for me from his own. I could have kissed him – well in fact I did. So that is how Sally, Diana and I stormed Cazorla bullring with the hay bursting out of the car, the sun beating down, Bossy at last finding something worth sniffing and all of us revelling in having a whole bullring, that iconic, powerful space, just for us. Sally and Diana who remember more "Corridas" than I will ever see, stood on the sand and talked famous matadors and bulls, "rejoneadores" and "ganaderias"(bull breeding farms) with the empty seats - and the rather astonished inhabitants of some apartments blocks around the Plaza de Toros, - looking down.

So we headed home with the one remaining bale of hay and bag of oats, our route tumbling down the mountainside to the steep and spectacular village of Tiscar. First we passed the Castle of the Black Rock teetering on the highest peak and overlooking the Sanctuary where the Virgin of Tiscar resides when she is not being carried over the mountain roads on a Romeria or spending her summer holidays in the neighbouring village of Quesada.

Every village has its "Romeria". The saint or virgin of the village is taken out into the country by oxen, on the shoulders of the faithful or on four wheels with large numbers of village following on foot or on horseback. There follows a day or two of partying, an enormous paella is served, a bar opens in the woods, there is usually a live band and dancing and horse games along the lines of a grown-up gymkhana. The origins of this custom are not clear. Some say it is linked to the "Rosemary for Remembrance" tradition, rosemary is "Romero" in Spanish, and certainly the walkers following the saint usually have sprigs of the herb on their walking staves. However the other theory is that it dates from the times when the Romans took their gods out to the fields for dancing and debauchery. Indeed, by the time the sun sets and things are cranking up, a lot of the Romerias I have been to are fairly Bacchanalian. The Virgin of Tiscar is actually carried across the mountain to the neighbouring village of Quesada in April where she is greeted by a shower of petals from all the balconies and she stays there until 29th of August before returning to her lonely sanctuary amid the towering rocks. Our road then descended pretty well vertically into the little hamlet of Don Pedro getting narrower and more tortuous by the minute. We managed to squeeze the car down tiny streets to the bottom of the village and leave the feed with the family who will look after me tomorrow night and then a sixteen-point turn, a lot of revving up the hill and we sped back down towards Hinojares and dinner at Pili's hotel.

121

＊

April 13th

Luqa's sadness and the silence of Don Pedro

Sun blazing down, deep blue sky, gentle breeze and the horses and I raring to go. Or so I thought. My two oats-on-wheels ladies and Bossy came to watch me pack Luqa with an extra high load for the narrow trail, my packing skills now honed to perfection and the whole operation taking about half the time it did two weeks ago. They drove away in a shower of gravel, planning a jolly good lunch with an old friend half-way home.

We set off across the campo, Penelope's route for today being untenable in its new guise as a busy paved mountain road. Besides, my way was so beautiful, the sweeping gorges and steep crumbly hillsides ranging from dusty pink to burnt umber and I rode along with a song in my heart until Luqa, my good boy, my hero, started acting the maggot. He would stop absolutely dead, planted in the middle of the track on the very end of his lead rope and refuse to take one step more. When I tried to ride round behind him to give him a slap on the bum he reversed and reversed and, when he got the chance, whipped round and tried to dash back the way we had come. I had to get off time after time and attempt to get him going again from the ground and in the end, only half an hour out of Hinojares, I tied them both up under a solitary tree and we all had a rest. It was clear what the problem was. Poor Luqa was telling me he had had enough. I could see it in his eyes. "WHY do we have to leave that place, I liked it there. WHERE are we going? WHEN will we stop going on and on? WHAT IS THE POINT?"

My two travelling companions were reacting very differently to this new experience. Bruma trundled along merrily on the off chance I might let her graze soon and if I didn´t she knew I would at lunchtime and she also knew that wherever we were going it would involve oats in the end and might even produce a handsome stallion to flirt with. Luqa thinks things through and was getting just a little sad and homesick and disorientated because we never seemed to arrive at our final destination. I fished around in the saddle bag until I found some of the carrots Diana and Sally had brought and spent about ten minutes shaving off tiny bits with my knife and letting them eat them from my hand. Then I led them forward, producing more snippets of carrots and lots of pats and encouraging noises, particularly that click in the back of the throat that every horse born in Spain recognises as loving communication. By the time we got to the questionable descent into the gorge, Luqa was focused on the trail in front and not what we had left behind and I mounted up thankfully because I did not fancy being trampled by iron shoes as we slithered down over the rocks.

We successfully negotiated the narrowest parts of the path, the pack on the taller horse clearing rocks and guard rails, and arrived in a deep valley with a rushing stream and a nightingale. It was hot and still, watched over by some charming little ruined farms, and we made a clatter like a troop of cavalry crossing a narrow wooden bridge. Down here, sheltered between the towering rocky slopes, was a settlement called Molino, apparently totally deserted, but Bruma stopped stock still by a little shrine to the Virgin and stared up at the roof of the house above us. Up there was a young man called Fermin, working away on the stonework. Yes, he told me, this had been his grandparents' house and his mother had lived in it as a child. He was re-building and renovating so he and his girlfriend could come and live down here, in the peaceful valley by the noisy stream. He was going to fix it up perfectly – it would be better than when his mother lived here, they had a 4x4 vehicle and solar power.

The track broadened and we climbed up and over some ridges, the mountain scape opening out before us dramatically, until the hamlet of Belerda lay ahead, one mountainside down from Don Pedro which is the "aldea" linked to the castle and sanctuary church of Tiscar. We found two nice troughs in Belerda which were very welcome for a long drink on this hot morning as was the pub which was packed with people including my hosts for the night, Juana and Angel Bautista Fernandez who had walked down from Don Pedro.

*

I had searched for somewhere for the three of us to stay in Tiscar and been introduced to Juana, a cosy middle aged woman of generous proportions, who managed the only two Casa Rurales in the hamlet of Don Pedro. Both houses belonged to people from Madrid who obviously had hugely inflated ideas of what you could ask a lone traveller and two horses to pay for one night. When they told Juana they would charge me €100 and what did she think they could ask for the horses, she hung up, had a word with her husband, Angel, and invited me to stay with them.

*

So I carried on up the mountain on a track that had been friendly sand for Penelope but was now cemented and pretty horrible to get iron-shod animals along. I dismounted early on and they struggled and slipped, their road studs useless on this particular surface. At one point Luqa completely lost his nerve and froze in the middle of the lane, all four legs trembling. I could only carry on leading Bruma up the steepest part and then tie her to a lamp post and return for him. Blessed relief to turn off that horrible slope into a whitewashed level alley that led around a couple of corners to Juana and Angel's house and tiny olive grove.

We couldn't have been made more welcome. Angel, who I realised had very poor eyesight, exuded kindness with every gesture. He took me to the little shady grove behind the house and organised a complicated system of bucket-carrying to offer the horses water. They had a free run of the place which was ringed by ancient walls and banks but I decided to keep a close eye on them and tie them up during the night as there was a delicious vegetable garden sharing the grove with the olive trees. The children, Nazaret aged ten and the twins Rocio and Cristina, two years younger, but, for their older sister I am sure, irritatingly taller and more robust and braver, were beside themselves with excitement to have horses in the back yard, getting to know them with a lot of squeaking and nervous commotion. These children have never even been in contact with a mule. I spent a lot of the afternoon dragging Bruma round and round the very small space with one girl at a time on board, smile stretching from ear to ear, ducking under the olive branches. However, when Angel had a go she went on strike and reversed, almost beheading him on a low branch. He was sweet and, bleeding copiously, said she was very "noble" and he understood! She was bored stiff by this time but I did not dare suggest a little trot around the village now I knew the dangers of those lethal glassy streets. All of this was supervised by granny, Maximiliana, to whom one felt the "more mules than hot dinners" rule applied.

I had the run of a cousin's empty house right beside theirs, old style, steps up, steps down between every room, holy pictures and whitewashed walls and blissfully cool on a hot afternoon. Juana brought me a plate of "arroz caldoso" with saffron and peas, wild mushrooms, artichokes, beans and a pork marrowbone. All the vegetables came from the garden in the olive grove which I hoped the horses had not yet discovered. It was surprisingly spicy and Penelope recounted eating the same dish in Tiscar. She divined that peppers with the seeds left in were the cause of the kick in the taste.

Penelope arrived in Tiscar, which she described as a *"Grimms Fairy Tale village"*, during the "matanza" or annual pig killing. Pretty well every house would have had a pig, fattened on scraps throughout the year to turn into hams and sausages, chorizo and black pudding. She describes the activity in the posada where she was staying, the whole family involved in the preparation for making "morcilla" or black pudding.

"We scrambled down a precipitous path to the river where the ladies of the posada were on their knees washing the coral coloured intestines in a misty blue pool. And by the time we had climbed home the intestines had beaten us to it and were cosily coiled up in a large earthenware crock. Such a scene of domestic industry I have seldom witnessed. The eldest son of the house, Hilario, was turning chopped onions simmering in olive oil in a gigantic black frying pan...his lovely young wife, Felicidad (Happiness), far gone with child, was washing tripe in a gigantic basin on the table...his elder sister, Paquita (engaged to an accordion player from Belerda) and her mother, Señora Barga (my hostess) were crisping pimientos in smoking oil for a minute a piece so they could afterwards be ground to powder: other women were cutting up onions, chopping parsley, peeling cloves of garlic and pounding peppercorns in a small brass mortar with a minute brass pestle. I was allowed to indulge in one of my favourite pastimes: blanching almonds."

Juana and Angel's neighbours, Segunda and Francisco who is known as "El Colorado", are a generation or two older than my hosts and remembered the Varga family who ran the posada. Señora Varga was a good seamstress and made lovely flouncy feria dresses for Segunda who lit up remembering the parties there used to be and the miles they would walk to get to them, never missing a gathering. Hilario, the onion fryer, was described by Penelope as handsome and El Colorado laughed.

"Handsome indeed he was – and he knew it. He was always washing and brushing and he loved bright clothes, like a peacock in reds and blues. And do you know, his son Hilarito, who was born in 1961 after that lady left, was a quiet chap but his grandson, Rosendo is just like his grandfather? His wife Felicidad, known as Feliza, was beautiful too. They live in Alicante now."

And the accordion player?

Great merriment .

"Oh yes, he is still around, still playing the squeezebox. What a character, his nickname is Pesca. He and Paquita live in Huesa [a neighbouring village]."

"There are no parties now," sighed Segunda, who probably has a wardrobe full of party dresses made by Señora Varga, kept just in case.

"And no pigs," added El Colorado. "Just the olives."

After the girls had serenaded me on their recorders and their Border Collie and small hairy yapping machine of uncertain origin had eaten up the rice remains, I set off to explore. I had an excellent guide in Penelope but I was also increasingly anxious about finding a way to climb out in the morning without breaking all my horses´ legs. My hosts assured me there was no way except the streets, but I was learning how quickly people deprived of any kind of animal transport forget the cutthroughs and pathways which are not suitable for cars.

Huffing and puffing I climbed up the little hamlet, feet pointing steeply to heaven, until I reached the old flour mill, in front of which were three little broken-down houses. The middle one had been the posada. This part of the village now appears totally deserted, the silence hanging like a question mark above the once bustling mill and bakers´ ovens. Here lived

Emiliano the baker, his wife Mari Carmen and the handsome baker´s boy whom Penelope had photographed with the bakery mule. They made bread for a village of four hundred souls, now reduced to forty. I found the exact spot where Penelope had taken a photo looking down on the posada, sunken and crumbling a little, the courtyards overgrown with wild roses and honeysuckle but not that changed in structure. I made my photo black and white like hers and studied them side by side. The real difference is that her picture had people in it. I had taken a photograph of...silence.

The little children of the posada had taken their extraordinary and exciting guest for a tour of the village as soon as she arrived so I followed in their footsteps and climbed up to the now famous "Cueva del Agua". It is a huge cavern which can only be reached via a rock tunnel where you bend double to get through. Emerging onto a wooden platform high above the cave floor, the noise of the water was deafening as it crashed twenty metres from the cave ceiling right down and across the vast space before launching itself into the abyss through a dazzling cleft in the rock below left. They used to have concerts here, recitals of Andalusian, Celtic, Flemish, Andean, Sephardic and Renaissance music, all sorts of melodies and rhythms resounding in the acoustics of this magical grotto when the waterfall was silenced in the summer drought, but, alas, in 2017 the dreaded "Health and Safety" gurus found even this remote and romantic spot and stopped the music.

Hundreds of people still come here from a radius of many kilometres for the feast of the Virgin on September 8th, presumably all filtered in one by one practically on their hands and knees through the little tunnel. Looking across the cave floor far below in the void from the high platform, I followed the remains of little wax candles with my eye up the rock face on the other side, among stalactites and stalagmites, where I spotted the dearest little Madonna in her safe rocky eyrie, from whence she had observed the comings and goings of centuries of visitors.

She is not the original Virgin of Tiscar though, so I left this entrancing grotto, crouched my way back out of the tunnel and started to climb past the remains of the Arab castle of Tíscar. In 1319 this was the last redoubt to be reconquered by Christians in the area. Struggling on up, I came to the Sanctuary where the main Madonna lives, if she hasn't left on her hollyers for Quesada. Beside this "Sanctuario" is a pilgrim hostel that serves very good rabbit stew to exhausted and footsore riders who are regretting leaving their horses two hundred metres down the hill. I did not strike on up the rocky path with the stations of the cross that led to the castle of the Black Rock. I could've but I reckoned if Penelope, a spring chicken sixteen years younger than me, hadn't bothered, I was not obliged to. And besides I was completely banjaxed.

The walk back down was truly beautiful, even though I seemed to be on the route that Penelope had described as *"the steepest stone path I had negotiated since riding over two Himalayan passes in Kathmandu..."* and now, turned into a glassy paved road, it was ten times worse. In spite of the scent of the jasmine, the green grey of the silvery olives interspersed with scarlet poppies and quince blossom, the ancient stone trough sprouting moss and carved faces and the general loveliness all around me, all I could think about was how to get my travelling companions out of here and over the pass tomorrow morning in one piece. There was no wifi here so my staunch companion, Google Earth, couldn´t help. Shanks´s pony just had to take me back and forth and up and down, behind deserted houses, through dead-end olive groves, braving the ubiquitous barking dogs until finally I found it! A teeny track that slithered past an old cottage and then opened up into a zigzag dirt trail, emerging far above at the Cueva del Agua. From there I could link with the Gran Ruta 7 which was where tomorrow´s ride would start! Elated I walked home in the dusk to tie each horse firmly up for the night and, with help from the girls who had by now finished their homework, to give them water and hay in their peaceful grove.

I visited Juana and Angel in their house next door. They sat at a central table which, if it had not been 25° outside, would surely have had a little stove of embers under the velvet table-cloth to keep the family cosy. On the walls were large photographs of their wedding and the childrens´ First Communions. Nazaret went and fetched her special album with photos of her posing in all her white frills with a horse that it transpired they had gone all the way to Cazorla to find as it was her dream on her special day to have her picture taken with a horse.

We talked about the sadness of this beautiful hamlet emptying of its people. When Juana was her daughters´ age in the 1980´s, the local school was packed and there were two buses that fetched the older children to secondary school in a town nearby. When her own three started their education, they were the only kids in the village and they were offered a home schooling teacher.

"But I wanted them to socialise with other youngsters, they were already isolated enough, so I drove them to school for two years. Now there are two more children in Don Pedro, just a total of five, so transport is provided. If they want qualifications they will have to go to Ubeda or Huesa or Quesada you know and they will not come back here, this place is dying. It is sad, so sad."

It seemed ineffably sad to me as the golden evening light backlit the tiny vineyard next door, framing the magnificent mountain backdrop in gilded leaves. There were cats soaking up the last of the sun's rays, Angel sat on the steps of an abandoned house playing with a neighbour's little grandson, visiting for the weekend, and an old lady in black hung her washing on an oleander bush. But the animals have already gone, no braying donkey, no "look, look, look I just laid an egg" from someone's hen house, no bells on the mountain as the goats were brought in for milking. These places die silently, that is the clue. Like the silence up at Penelope's posada.

However, my whimsical conclusions were soon cut short by the arrival of the very un-whimsical granny, Maximiliana. She came to see me in my house, proffering a branch of a bay tree for good luck and protection from evil spirits on my travels. Solid, not very tall but completely square, dressed from head to toe in black except for her hair which was an unexpected shade of maroon, she reckoned if interviews were going on, she was the one to talk to. Indefatigable, as are so many Andalusian women of a certain age, she had a lot to tell me:

Her name is Maximiliana Moreno Cantisano. She has three daughters and a son which was a small family back then. Her friend Pura had eight. Only her daughter Juana lives in Don Pedro but she has a widowed daughter in Belerda where she goes down to sleep every night in case the daughter might be lonely. She remembers when Penelope came. They had a shop then run by Eulogia and Prudencio. It sold everything and the posada children took Penelope there. [They did indeed, to buy throat pastilles]. And there was mass every day with Friar Jaime, that's all gone now – which may be why the village is in such a poor state, not enough masses. [Penelope would agree totally on this].

Maximiliana, as a girl, went every year to pick grapes in France. Her whole family made the annual pilgrimage so they could feed the children. She also worked in the olives up over the Tiscar pass, walking there daily, leaving before dawn and earning 30 pesetas a day – about 18 cents of a Euro in today's money. She remembers getting measles from the olive trees – oh yes, they can give you the measles. She walked home and they wrapped her in a red blanket for a day and a night to 'get out the measles'.

Maximiliana disappeared for a minute or two and returned with more bay branches. I tried to explain the complications of pack saddles and vegetation but she was hurt and upset, this was for me and my horses' protection. In the end I accepted her gift and, right until the end of my ride, the scent of crushed bay leaves would drift up every time I opened my pack paniers, and those evil spirits didn't get a look in.

Night fell and the ancient house wrapped around me. The old-fashioned bed had a deep channel in the middle which any couple would have rolled into within minutes of climbing in. An inevitable cuddle like that and you'd be plugged in in no time! The numerous children of friend Pura and the rest were probably due to beds like this in which I half woke, half dreamed the night away. The happy and sad times of the house were present in its dirt floors and steep stairs as the nightingales saturated the horses dozing in the moonlight, their song drowning out the occasional barking of the dogs.

*

I returned a few months later to ride with José on his horses in another part of the park and called in to see my friends in Don Pedro. A few days earlier Maximiliana and Juana had been busy making preserves of the produce of their fruit trees and vegetable garden. Full of plans and leaving everything ready for final bottling next day, the old lady went to bed and never woke up. I rode in to find a tearful, diminished little family, telling me how she had been looking forward to seeing me again. "We miss her love" they said.

Clockwise from top: Leaving Hinojares, A family ride, Mine and PC´s photos of the Posada and bakery, then and now.

*

April 14th

Scary paths and guardian foxes

Palm Sunday morning and the "help" giving me the hee-bie-jeebies with a lot of enthusiastic but inexpert brushing under the horses' bellies and small fingers going into their cavernous mouths along with the carrots. The whole Bautista Fernandez family rose early to see me off up my very successful steep dirt path out of the village as the sun rose, though I had a feeling Angel had every intention of going back to bed for his Sunday lie in as soon as I was out of sight. Climbing hard, the horses put their chests into it, Luqa carrying the pack again as I thought he might like another day of not being in charge. The horse in the lead will automatically take responsibility for the herd, however small, and it is therefore much more tiring for that horse, minding out for lions on the others' behalf. I told them how lucky they were that I hadn't spent three days in Tiscar feasting on four courses of different parts of the pig at almost every meal as Penelope had. She even consumed pig's brain's grilled on the embers for her last breakfast. I bet La Marquesa was puffing harder than them up this bit.

We crested the Tiscar pass within an hour and stopped to

take a picture of the view. Black Rock Castle and the Sanctuary on their dramatic crags were backlit to the east by the rising sun and southwards, between the rocks down over Don Pedro, we glimpsed the folding, fading, chalky pink hills we had climbed up yesterday, the wide hazy plains disappearing into infinity beyond.

Now we were in traditional mountain country, forested on the lower slopes, scrubby bushes further up and bare rock on the tops. The Cazorla Natural Park is the largest of its kind in Spain, measuring over two thousand square kilometres and filled with water sources. Two major rivers rise here, the Guadalquivir and the Segura. There is a high waterfall, the Chorro Gil, a big reservoir lake, El Tranco, and myriad brooks and waterways. All this abundance of water and uninterrupted space means it is packed with wildlife and, when I was working in Spain in the eighties, we were all glued to a television series, "El Hombre y La Tierra", (Man and The Earth) made by a charismatic naturalist called Felix Rodriguez de la Fuente. He was the David Attenborough of Spain and we never missed a programme. He died on his fifty-second birthday in a light plane accident and I had only recently found out that he lived, worked and filmed almost entirely in the Sierra de Cazorla, so this was something of a pilgrimage for me.

Two golden eagles, perched a few metres away, watched us as we crossed the high pass, like gatekeepers to the real mountains. At this point, Penelope's and my way diverged as she had taken what is now a narrow main road to Quesada and I continued along a glorious route that Jose Coronado had told me about. Buried in my pocket was my phone with his Wikiloc map, ready to get irritated if we went off-piste.

137

We dropped over the lip of what looked like a precipice but actually had a trail just wide enough for two horses abreast clinging to the cliff edge. There really was no way we could take a wrong turn here and stay alive. We wound down and along the contours of the spectacular mountain, the path diminishing in width so Luqa´s pack jostled against us and the rock. Far, far below to our left, beyond the vast, yawning gorge, were endless olive groves, the trees looking like full stops. Pressing close to us on the right-hand side, a sheer limestone wall, top invisible as it disappeared into a realm my craning neck could not decipher. This would not have been a ride for Penelope who suffered from vertigo.

Adding to the excitement, after last week´s rain, mountain streams crashed off the cliff across our path before committing suicide over the edge into the bottomless abyss. Bruma did an emergency stop at every one and then launched herself in a bundle, clearing each little torrent by metres. By this time I had Luqa following behind as there really was no room for him and his pack beside us and almost every time the little mare leapt I had to let go of his lead rope - or risk getting pulled off and tumbling away into the gorge. By now, dismounting and remounting was really not an option, nor was turning my ride horse round to recapture the pack pony so, non-vertiginous as I am myself, it put the fear of God into me too. After a sweaty-palmed hour, our track started getting wider and a few strag-gly pine trees appeared, growing between us and the drop, and everything felt safer. Penelope had exactly the same experience searching these mountains, fruitlessly as it turned out, for the source of the River Guadalquivir.

"Never before have I realised how friendly, how almost human,

trees can be in the high sierra. Never again shall I say anything nasty about conifers. I have no head for heights so whenever the path led over bare rock, with God knows what dreadful precipice falling away into the mist, I was petrified. But when it led back among the pine trees I felt perfectly safe. They seemed to receive me with open arms and to say "Come into us, we will protect you from the abyss, we will keep you safe."

Now we started to see animals – or maybe I just hadn't been looking anywhere but at each faltering step up until then. There were mountain goats, like large chamois, on the same trail as us, trotting along ahead. Obviously even they are not going to venture off THIS path! As the forest increased around us we saw handsome red squirrels and roe deer. But the most memorable were two foxes who kept pace with us behind for a long while and then nipped past, inches from the horses' legs, and carried on up a little side alley out of sight. I think their names might have been Gabriel and Raphael and they were going into the wood to take off their foxy disguises and shake out their wings. Mission accomplished.

We reached a viewpoint called the Collado Zamora, ringed with peaks over two thousand metres high, with glistening snow on the top. From here we looked down and down to a sea of olives, hundreds of thousands, stretching far across the great rolling plain of Ubeda to Jodar and the Sierra Magina where, God (and Gabriel and Raphael) willing, I would be in a week's time.

Up here there was a forest hut or refuge, where the weary walker could pass the night which I made a mental note of. I was still planning "La Ruta de Penelope", the official walking route I hoped might come out of this adventure, and today's journey would be too long for all but the most experienced hikers (or very tall Dutchmen) to do in one go. While the horses grazed in a little mountain meadow, I drearily drank my protein powder mixed with water, and thought that even Penelope managed to organise more interesting, though somewhat unusual, picnics, such as leftover tortilla, almonds and a lemon. I was so involved in finding out about her, mapping my route and making sure the horses were fed, I tended to neglect my own midday sustenance and brought the protein drinks with this in mind. Otherwise, taking advantage of the very occasional shop along my way, I would have had to think two or three days ahead for my own lunches, and I just couldn't be bothered. However, I always regretted this when the time came to stop and refuel, soaking up some impressive view or other which would have been better suited to a spread of sandwiches, cheese, chorizo, fruit and maybe a little glass of something.

After lunch we continued along broad forest paths, a long and gradual descent, wafts of wild lavender and rosemary mixing with the scent of pine. Here we started meeting tourists, which was a bit of a shock! First the hikers, mostly garbed in brand new brilliantly coloured Decathlon hiking outfits, good for mountain rescue to find you but guaranteed to terrorise any shy animals peering out of the forest. These good folk were puffing uphill on their poles and gasped a greeting but did not stop and chat – a first for this ride when everyone we met along the way wanted a conversation. Then came cars, creeping up the hills stuffed with families, faces set in "making the most of the holiday Sunday" mode. Some smiled and took pictures of us, some pushed by showing clearly that we were in the way and not the sort of wildlife they had come to see. By the time we had been walking downhill for an hour there were walkers, cyclists and cars round every corner - we were in the middle of tourist turmoil!

A word at this point about cyclists. Why does everyone seem to have it in for them? I find them friendly and polite and even when they are in total agony grinding up a steep hill they always manage a grunt of greeting. Why they put themselves through it remains a mystery to me but they probably think the ease I have going up the same hills on my four legged cycles is totally negated by our inability to go "WHEEEEEEE!" at high speed when we come to the downhills. I have a lot of time for cyclists, even though those lycra shorts can be a little distracting... Not the same can be said for carloads of hollering, snotty kids, exhausted whey-faced mothers and the fathers, expressionless and raging, obviously considering just driving over the edge with the whole fecking lot. I do kind of sympathise but not enough to forgive the one who drove past us, without a glance, not giving an inch as we squashed as best we could on the side of the drop. He actually scraped against the pack shunting us further towards the brink and accelerated away.

"I hope yer next shite is a hedgehog!" I hollered after him, Dublin style.

As we continued down, the build-up of "turistas" became ridiculous and the reason for their concentration in this part of the forest, evident. We were approaching the source of the River Guadalquivir, that great waterway that flows for more than six hundred kilometres roughly east southeast through the iconic cities of Cordoba and Sevilla before reaching the sea in the estuary at Sanlucar de Barrameda, watering the wetlands of another natural park, La Doñana. Penelope, searching on two occasions for the birthplace of this river, in foul weather and braving her vertigo, had not succeeded in finding it. But then she did not have the advantage of signs along every trail and track pointing the way. When I got there the trippers were three deep but I took a picture of my companions in front of a sign saying "Nacimiento (Birthplace) del Rio Guadalquivir" where the water gushed from the rock and we continued on our way with the little blue-green stream bustling along down to our right.

The end of today's ride seemed interminable, the last ten hot kilometres of nearly forty. It was a broad track, suitable for cars, and both Luqa and Bruma were really flagging in spite of now being incredibly fit. Like me, I think they were flagging from boredom. At one point I was sure we had reached the turn-off to their stables and my camping place but the forgotten phone in my pocket gave a loud "wah wah", horses stopped dead, knowing what this meant and we returned to our boring old trail, at which point we heard the encouraging chirrup from a satisfied phone. At long last we reached the campsite where I would spend the night and I tied the horses up and unloaded what I reckoned were the necessities for a night's camping before I went to leave the horses. There seemed to be an awful lot on the floor of "Reception" after I had done the drop. There was a sleeping bag and a sleeping mat, my little gas stove, mug and plate and instant tea and soup and army rations, my camping towel and an enormous bottle of mosquito repellent , my leather "bota" of whiskey, my warm poncho as an extra blanket, a head torch and then of course a small rucksack of clothes.

A little more than a kilometre on along the woodland road

we came to Cristobal´s peaceful settlement. He was lying in a hammock beside the turquoise stream that would become the great river, reading a book when we arrived. There was a sense of peace down there, his other horses dozed in their corrals as we unloaded the remaining pack and tack and stored it in his stables and my horses drank deep and long from a hollowed out tree trunk that served as a trough with water straight out of the stream. They had a shady corral all to themselves and I left them happily munching to the sound of the water.

Cristobal pointed out a little path that went through the woods on the bank of the brook and I walked in on the campsite from the far end, rather fascinated as, believe it or not, I had never been to an official camping establishment before. There were camper vans and tents and then permanent wooden huts in one of which I was delighted to find myself. It was fabulous and very cheap and I had an enormous bed with sheets to put on it so bye bye sleeping bag and mat. Two towels were provided plus a bathroom with solar heated water, lights in every room, solar again, and a perfectly good kitchen with gas stove, microwave and oven. I had no need to delve into my emergency rations because there was a restaurant attached to the site serving food and drink in abundance! All my bags and packages hauled there from reception were completely superfluous.

The little camping restaurant provided me with home-made meatballs, tomato and garlic salad and a glass of verdejo wine and I even splashed out on an ice cream, something I only eat about once a year on momentous occasions!

*

April 15th

A cabin by a newborn river

Sleeping in a little wooden house was definitely more comfortable and welcoming than the usual 21st century tourist accommodation in southern Spain known as "Casas Rurales", the title denoting that they are for the use of tourists. In 1961 Penelope remarked upon the enthusiasm with which Spanish women approached cleanliness, sweeping and scrubbing their houses constantly and beating their clothes relentlessly on the rocks of every stream she passed.

"Women never seem to stop washing in Spain"

I suppose that in those days they were fighting a battle against dust and dirt and disease in houses with clay floors and wooden-raftered roofs, shared with the livestock and a variety of creepy crawlies. However, the battle continues to this day and the women are winning! Cleanliness is no longer next to Godliness, it is way ahead.

In the modern Liquorice Allsorts houses, walls, ceilings, floors, and furniture have shiny surfaces where no dirt dares cling. Smooth plastic or ceramic wipe-able everythings are the order of the day and tiles, tiles, tiles. Nary a whisker of your dog would dare settle and a grain of sand is visible from five metres. As soon as the Town Hall has a bit of money, the streets in these country villages are primped and paved and decorated so that, not only can your horse not take a dump or your dog hoist a leg, but on a wet day all three of you are likely to come a purler on the marble-smooth surfaces. This means that the usual impeccably presented tourist accommodation one comes across in Andalusia does not so much welcome you with open arms as give you a sharp elbow in the ribs.

So it was with some reluctance I left my cosy hut by the nascent Guadalquivir, having slept in until nine in the morning, latest ever. This being Spain, country of the long holiday lie-in, none of my fellow campers were moving around when I set off, laden with the bags and bundles I would not need after all, through the woods to the horses. The river was jewel-blue and the sun warm, belying the snow we saw on the high peaks and in the shady ditches beside our long descent yesterday.

I found my companions lying down in their little corral, covered in yellow and orange butterflies. Luqa was squinting at half a dozen perched on his nose and Bruma, eyes blissfully shut, was wearing them mostly behind her ears. We dawdled over to the river where they drank deeply of Guadalquivir, a recent vintage, apparently none the worse for their forty kilometre adventure yesterday. Then back to the paddock with wheat straw to eat, courtesy of Cristobal.

Born in Cataluña, Cristobal looks like a wiry woodsman or horseman, not carrying the extra few kilos most men of middle age in Andalusia tend to. When he was a young lad, his uncle kept up to thirty horses in the seaside town of Blanes, Girona, for the tourists to ride. He used to rush off after school every

145

day to help and was soon hooked on horses. His "real" job was as a teacher of mechanics and electricity and he also ran a gym in Blanes. At the age of twenty-nine, he left all that behind and took off, as he puts it "for an adventure" and that was how he ended up in these southern mountains. He learnt Forestry and Environmental studies in the college of the Natural Park of the Sierra de Segura and then worked as a firefighter. At the same time, he started acquiring a horse or two and at weekends he rode extensively over the hills and trails until he knew them all. Turning two mares out to graze in wild lands near a lake, they met a stallion and were soon in foal and that was the nucleus of his little herd which he has run as a trekking outfit for twenty-five years.

Apart from his accent, it is hard to say why one would know straight away that Cristobal was not originally from Andalusia, perhaps just the fact that he talked about "taking a sabbatical" from the horses this year which would not be a local concept. Either you are going on with the business or not.

When he rented the little strip of land which is his glade, there was nothing except the stream and the trees. He has built, with wood, stables and tack room, a wood store, four corrals and his own house. Everything is finished off perfectly, the cabin he lives in has an enormous fireplace upon which he toasted me my breakfast, and a kitchen with all mod-cons including a washing machine, running off a generator and solar. It is all so simple, he has everything he could want, right beside his horses. No car but, as he puts it:

"Someone is always going somewhere and I get a lift"

Every detail is thought out and - yes, that is another clue to where he came from - there are no higgledy-piggledy junk dumps of items, kept just-in-case or because no one has bothered to get rid of them. The clearing in the forest is…clear.

As we ate our breakfast and he showed me his wonderful Catalan fireside toaster on a swivel for toasting huge slices of local bread on both sides, he told more of his plans for this trek-free year.

What will he do?

"My carpentry, I want to make things and work with wood again, and lie in my hammock and read. I want to sit by the fire on chilly days and listen to music. Then I have planned a trip to Morocco with friends and maybe to see someone else in Mallorca. I would like to take a longer spell away, maybe a month, so I have found a girl who is going to the forestry school where I studied and wants to keep her horses here. This works well because she will pop in each day and can keep an eye on my animals too"

Meanwhile, today he was going to finish making a table and stitching up some leather saddlebags before retiring to his hammock over the stream. My pack saddle was taken apart and photographed from every angle and Cristobal reckoned, if he could find someone to make the metal base, he could copy the rest, and I am sure he could!

There are some magical days and people who make life seem straightforward and show you that, once you step aside from what you "should" do and look around, all sorts of wonderful plans and adventures seem possible.

A few kilometres even deeper into the forest, along a deserted road skirting the high mountains that separate the park from Cazorla town, is the Parador de Cazorla. Now a swanky hotel, in Penelope's time this was Franco's hunting lodge. Set above a deep valley looking away westward towards the endless layers of blue hills fading to silvery grey, it is an impressive building with a large terrace running the length of the front from which you could presumably spot any game ambling across the panorama. Snuggled in amongst the pines and rocks with heather and gorse growing up to the back door, it could almost be a Scottish lodge or a Bavarian Jagdschloss but the windows and doors, opening onto terraces and lawns leading to a swimming pool, would not perhaps be part of the essentials for a winter-shooting season further north. A wide sunlit courtyard which would once have housed his horses and hounds is now a tradesman's delivery spot and car park – don't you hate it when something so exciting is transformed into something so mundane?

There are plenty of photos of Franco on shooting parties in Cazorla and elsewhere. One memorable panorama is of his immediate family grouped in a wide field. There are twenty-eight of them, the gentlemen favouring plus fours and boots that buckle up the outside, flat caps or broad-brimmed homburg hats. The ladies, sensible tweed coats and skirts and stylish felt hats with a tilt and a feather. Centre stage is Franco, baggiest plus fours of all, just a little shorter than everyone else, looking avuncular and thrilled skinny with himself and his family, the new aristocrats. The most extraordinary part of this picture, however, is the large field they are standing in which appears to be planted with strange dumpy plants as far as the eye can see. The caption explains that this is 1959 and the group in the picture had shot more than four thousand six hundred partridge, laid out all around them.

Well, Generalisimo – partisans? partridges? Hmmm.

Rumour has it that Franco, like the Fuehrer, had only one testicle. Is this a prerequisite for dictatorship? Did anyone count Mussolini's?

In the 1960's, Franco's regime had become somewhat more liberal and he was less the strict dictator and more the elder statesman. Penelope met people who really thought of him as a saint but this could have been a biased point of view as she was normally conversing with the good churchgoing population, not taking into account that if your family did not go to church in the Franco years, your child could be excluded from school, among other subtle punishments. A priest in Ubeda told her how the General always spent the night in prayer in front of the blessed sacrament before taking a decision, but then this priest had had a terrible experience in the Civil War at the hands of the Republicans, seeing his Carmelite friars dying from being tortured and only being spared himself because he ran a school for poor boys. He likened those years to the Roman persecutions in early Christian times. Others told her that Franco had saved the country and preserved the Catholic faith and that the people were poor but happy and everyone had enough to eat, which is not the story I was being told by people who remembered the 1950's and 60's.

Penelope claimed she knew very little about the Spanish Civil War and could only judge the small corner where she was in 1961.

"Having spent six months in fascist Italy in 1928 and lived in Berlin for three months in 1933...the present regime in Spain has created a very different atmosphere to that in the hundred per-cent fascist countries of Italy and Germany before World War 2. Naturally there is known to be a certain amount of anti-clericalism

149

among people whose husbands or fathers were shot by the nation-alists and who would rather die than darken the doors of a church but I didn't myself come across any of these, whereas in Italy every other man I sit next to in a train or a country bus hates the church and there is an aggressively anti-clerical atmosphere up and down the country which is very unpleasant"

During the decade when Penelope visited, Spain was to become the fastest-growing economy in the world after Japan! Wages were low, strikes were forbidden and regulations negligible. Because of the low taxes, foreign countries started investing in Spain. A prime example is the once-sleepy coastal village of Benidorm where the package holiday was born in the 60's. It is a shame this prosperity took so long to filter down through the rural communities, leaving them to continue their mass-exodus from the villages for another decade.

In 2019 those who wanted to tell me that Franco was not all bad spoke in low voices and cautiously. The Civil War is still present in many people's memories and in the village where I live there are two groups of old fellas who never hang out on the same corner of the square. Most of them are a generation on from the Civil War but tales of family betrayals and neighbours shooting neighbours are still alive, if only faintly. Now there is definitely a strong swing of public opinion against those Franco years, and they have removed his remains from the seriously spooky Valley of the Fallen, an enormous Basilica built into the mountain with a great cross above and the certain knowledge that all around in the hillside are the bodies of the Republican prisoners who died building it. At its heart, in solitary arrogant pomp, lay Franco, the only resident, among thirty-three thou-sand dead, not killed in the war. Francoists would go there as a pilgrimage and I was taken years ago by one of them whose fanaticism added to the nasty taste that ominous place left in my mouth.

Living in modern Spain, the only act of Franco's that affects (and irritates) me is the hours we keep. During World War 2 he put Spain's clocks forward an hour in solidarity with his Nazi friends in Berlin. And there they have remained! So we are in the wrong time zone with winter dark mornings and no early summer dawns. Even in June it doesn't get light until about seven and then the endless light evenings mean we all have supper about ten at night and the neighbours' darling little children can still see to play football outside my house after that.

I left the horses and Cristobal to their world of butterflies and water wagtails and wandered back to the campsite where the other campers were stirring, many moving out as this was Monday morning and not all of them would stay on for the whole Easter week. A young family in a camper van, Ester and Luis, with children, Maite and Leon, approached and quizzed me about my adventure, having seen me pass on the road with the horses yesterday. Luis spoke good English which he had studied in his home town of Burgos and one of the books they had read was "Two Middle-Aged Ladies in Andalusia". This was the very first Spanish person I had met who had any idea about the existence of the book so, of course, I was now family! Invited to lunch I was fed and questioned simultaneously, something everyone here is very good at – which usually leaves me miles behind on the eating stakes as I am doing all the talking.

Ester and Luis and their kids are part of the generation

of Spanish who live every spare moment out in the hills or on the beach, on a bike or a canoe, walking, climbing or riding. People here bracket themselves into two categories of preference for their holidays, "Mar o Montaña" - Sea or Mountains, (which really means any countryside not on the coast). With six Natural Park visits under their belts, my friends were in Cazorla Park for the first time and definitely came under the "Montaña" category. The climate means that almost every weekend of the year there is an exodus from the cities to enjoy the great outdoors, and what a great outdoors it is. Spain is the most mountainous country in Europe after Switzerland and Northern Spain started the trend for marked walking and mountain biking paths several decades ago. There are "Via Ferrata" (lines and metal rungs with hand and footholds on rock faces to make climbing accessible for all), and marathons, cross-country runs and sheer mountain-bike trails every weekend. The villages of Andalusia even have exercise apparatus for their older inhabitants about a kilometre walk outside the centre to keep the senior citizens on the move. Without the drudgery of hard daily physical work the ordinary Spanish people are fine sportsmen and women. On the world stage Spain produces top footballers, tennis players, cyclists, basketball players, motorcyclists, Americas Cup sailors and Formula One drivers as a matter of course. I personally, have found a big difference with first time riders on a horse if they are Spanish. They have an instinctive natural balance which other nationalities do not necessarily share. Penelope saw it too.

"I was fascinated watching two boys on a trotting donkey stallion having a wrestling match....I never cease to admire the wonderful balance of these Andalusians. They are equally at home

sitting forwards or backwards or sideways on a trotting or galloping animal and I believe that without any preliminary training they could ride a horse over the largest showjump."

After an exhausting bike race with Maite and Leon, I reluctantly turned down an invitation to yet more food and drink and went back to study my map for the tricky ride tomorrow and to check, for the nineteenth time, that I still had the key to the bullring.

*

April 16th

The big zig zag to bullring heaven

I was nervous about today's traverse over the fourteen-hundred metre rock wall between Cazorla town and its Natural Park. The road route, which I had taken in the car with Sally and Diana on our feed delivery run, would add many kilometres so it was "over the top" or nothing.

*

Back in February, when I was desperately looking for horse accommodation in the town of Cazorla, a friend, Jon Addis of the seven-league legs, had volunteered to join me so he could try out the trails. Everyone I asked said the way I wanted to bring my horses at this stage was impossible but Jon, who likes to walk and has a horsey wife so knows what our intrepid Andalusian mounts can and can't cope with, was the ideal person to send out on recces while I paced the streets down in the valley. So, on Valentine's Day, when he should of course have been at home wining and dining said wife (did I feel a twinge of guilt? Did I heck. I was a complete obsessive by this time about my

"PLAN"), I drove him to the far side of the mountain range. It was a frosty morning, with good piney scents and sparkling distances, and his remit was to plot a route on foot that would work for one woman and two horses, either ridden or led, one with a laden pack saddle. When he marched successfully down into town hours later, he brought the good news, the bad news and a mass of photos of narrow paths, woodland trails, rocks blocking routes and grassy dells. It all looked fairly possible except for the last rather precipitous descent on a miniscule path with big rock steps and jutting sides that might not allow the pack saddle through. So, the morning we were due to drive home, we scrambled up from the Cazorla town side and investigated another possibility which was a great zigzag descent over steep and stony meadowland, dropping one hundred metres in just over a quarter of a kilometre. Not sure what angle that is but our zigs and our zags would have to be long ones.

*

Now the day had come to actually ride it I felt fairly confident about the part I had seen with my own eyes but for the rest, the first two or three hours, I could only follow Jon's instructions and try and avoid the bits of the mountain where, on Google Earth, the little walking-men figures were wearing ropes and hard hats.

It started well with Cristobal guiding me up the "Camino del Oso", the path of the bear, on his priceless pony, Pitufo. Originally used for hauling logs in the forest, Pitufo is as strong as two full-sized horses and he came out of the dell by the river like a firework rocket, not having been ridden for some time due to his owner's sabbatical. We raced along behind him, his little backside resembling a jetpack, legs pounding like pistons. After half an hour of ascending through the woods, Pitufo's jetpack ran low on gas and we sauntered past without breaking our stride, Luqa looking so superior, as he quietly reminded the little stocky fella of the tortoise and the hare. Just short of the Parador, Cristobal turned for home and we continued on, climbing up the east-facing pinewood trails in the morning sun beneath the Piñon del Rey or Peak of the King. Emerging from the trees we came to a magnificent corniche-style path, hugging the mountain to our right with great canyons and gorges below left. Before we actually stepped upon it, I took an executive decision and dismounted, leading my ride horse, Luqa, just behind me and leaving Bruma at the back, praying she had the sense not to try and barge up alongside the other horse. To keep her on the straight and narrow, I hooked her long lead rope through Luqa's stirrup but did not tie it. If the very worst happened to one of them there was no sense in taking their companion with them. On these occasions I was in a quandary as to the best plan of action because Bruma, completely loose, does tend to dive at succulent, almost out-of-reach morsels of mountain vegetation, probably knowing exactly what she can and can't risk but putting the heart across me.

We walked along with breath-taking vistas stretching away to the west and once again I longed for someone to take our picture on days like this, the more extraordinary days of our journey. My head by now was full of images of dramatic mountain-scapes and curving, climbing, plunging paths where these eight little hoofs had taken us, but no one else would ever see how it really was on the tricky bits because the horses had me handicapped. It was impossible, when carefully riding or leading and reassuring the horses, to get far enough away from them to include more than a saddle or an ear in my photos of the view; and only an awful eejit would ask them to wait a minute and pose while said eejit rushed away to get a good vantage point.

Our path continued for several kilometres, fairly level, beautifully cambered, in places with big stones placed along the outside edge, always winding in and out of the vertical folds of the high mountain on our right. This was most definitely an ancient way, once taking travellers and pedlars, merchants and muleteers, flocks and herds between the markets of Cazorla town and the infinite grazing of the sierras. I remembered the shepherd, Rufino, who would walk his flocks here all the way from Pedro Martinez to give them the benefit of Cazorla pasture. We emerged onto a mountain meadow, high, high above our final destination and then plunged back into cool pine woods where we found an old stone trough with a spring flowing through it for a pause and a long drink followed by bubble-blowing while the two-legged member of the team climbed back on board. When we did come to the zigzag descent back to civilisation, I was glad I had investigated it before and decided we could do it because, from the top of a horse, it looked even steeper. However, we managed fine and were soon across the main road in the olive groves below Cazorla, a riot of colour since the recent rain. Wild sweet peas vied with rampant red clover and myriad lupins like bruises in the tree shadow with the great scarlet splashes of poppies winning of course, as they always do. Turning to look back up at our descent, beside the castle of La Iruela clinging to the rocky slopes by its stone toenails, it did look rather amazing that we had come down there.

One last nervous check on the bullring key and we trotted across the level landscape arriving almost opposite our destination. In fact the great metal doors were open and one of the council lorries was in there filling up with water. I asked if they came often, thinking of the risk of horses getting out or my stuff disappearing but they assured me that this was their last working day before Easter. There was just one inhabitant of the bullring, they told me, who might be a bit of trouble, but that person was out right now.

I was fed up as I knew it was bound to be some old lady clean-freak, living in one of the little houses inside the enclosure who would probably complain if I dropped a straw or, heaven forfend, one of the horses had a pee near her house. I was due to stay in Cazorla for several days and had looked forward to a free hand with the horses and their routine.

For the first time on my trek, I bathed the horses with a hosepipe. I had been reluctant to do it before and use up people's precious water supply but I reckoned the Ayuntamiento de Cazorla wouldn't miss a few litres. Once turned out in the bullring they couldn't get over the expanse of prime rolling sand. They walked round and round and round, buckling at the knees ready to go down and then changing their minds and moving on again. Eventually each found his or her perfect spot and a veritable orgy of backscratching, sweat-scraping, gyrating and revolving went on, weary legs waving in the air.

Penelope rode into Cazorla from the other end of town, having spent time in Quesada to the south. I planned on visiting that little town from here as it had turned out to involve a lot of main-road riding from Tiscar and no accommodation for the horses. Under a stormy sunset, La Marquesa had slithered down the treacherous muddy slope from a high watchtower on the soaring crags above the town, passing Castillo La Yedra,(Ivy Castle), a dramatic Moorish edifice tucked into the steep mountainside, guardian of the southern entry to Cazorla. Beneath them was the half-ruined church of Santa Maria. In 1961 it was just a wide-open roofless space where local women gathered to hang their washing to dry beneath the fine Renaissance walls and to chat out of the wind on winter days. Penelope was told that the French had destroyed the church but there was more to it than that.

With time on my hands and my goods and chattels safely installed in a hotel near the bullring, I walked across town, the streets gradually narrowing down to tiny alleyways until they opened onto the Plaza Santa Maria. This square is sandwiched on three sides by the mountains, Castillo La Yedra to the south and Peña de los Halcones or Falcons´Peak and nearly two thousand metres of Gilillo Peak towering to the north and east. In the walls of the great roofless Renaissance church was a the tourist office so I took the official tour feeling that Penelope´s conclusion on the history of Santa Maria – that it was all the fault of Napoleon – could not be the full story.

It turned out to be an incredible tale of what I believe would once have been called "vainglory" starting in 1534 when King and Emperor, Carlos V of Spain and his faithful secretary, Francisco de Cobos, decided they wanted to build a big and beautiful church to advance their power, riches and influence in Cazorla and, let´s face it, show off a bit. There was only one problem, squinched between the mountains as the town

159

was, and still is, there simply wasn't room. The only open space available was occupied by the busy little Rio Cerezuelo that rushes down from the hills and straight through the middle of the ancient city. However, if you are an ambitious king with an equally ambitious sidekick in Señor Cobos, you just bring in one of the greatest architects of that era, Andres de Vandelvira, and ask him to channel the whole river down a level and build a vaulted underground tunnel for it to pass through, thus freeing up enough space for a large Plaza and the construction of a magnificent church.

Our tour took us down and along the "boveda" or vault containing the river, all one hundred and twenty three metres of it. It is an extraordinary construction of deep excavation, angled and curved stones and great pillars that have been holding the hurrying, bustling, splashing little river in place for nigh on five hundred years. The noise of the water is deafening but, standing above ground, you would never know what is happening beneath your feet. It must have cost billions in today's terms and yet, somehow, the stunning and beautiful church was never finished, almost as if the arrogance that built it was recognised - and disapproved of - by a higher power. In 1614, just as the final touches were being put to the roof, there was a freak storm and half the Falcons' Peak washed straight down on top of the church. The rushing waters of the trapped Rio Cerezuelo burst up through the tunnel entrance, rising to over three metres throughout the square and taking great chunks of Santa Maria church with them. As if that wasn't enough, still unfinished, Napoleon's troops took against it in the 18th century, as Penelope reported, and bombarded it particularly viciously in retaliation for Cazorla's stubborn stand against them

160

and then set fire to it. Finally, Franco bombed it in the 1930's, though obviously, in 1961, the locals omitted to tell Penelope this as Franco was still rather the man of the month back then.

I retraced my steps across town through the minute streets. With the unwavering spatial awareness of Spanish drivers, the locals were not deterred from tearing through in their cars, skinning the knuckles of any pedestrian who did not leap onto a doorstep or dodge into another alley in time. Astonishingly, some of them were two way streets which meant that the un-suspecting tourists on foot frequently found themselves in the middle of a game of chicken between the motorists.

This was the way Penelope must have been led by the children she met by the Santa Maria Church who took her to the posada where she and La Marquesa would stay for the next few days. I found the sharp corner and steep cobbles leading to it, where the mare slipped and fell down, twice, due to worn horseshoes but, tempting as it was, I decided to go back to my horseless hotel and investigate further in the morning.

Clockwise from top: Views from Collado Zamora, Cristobal and Pitufo, beside the Guadalquivir.

162

*

April 17th

The enchanted posada

Happy horses, sunny bullring, but where was the bottle of whiskey, courtesy of Sally, that I had left with the horse feed we delivered here a few days ago? In between tending to such important details, so far as the horses were concerned, as hay and oats and water buckets, all to be transferred into the inner sanctuary of circular, silent sand, I puzzled about my unopened bottle of grog.

This was a simple "Plaza de Toros" with just a yard and a trough between the main gates and access to the ring. Spectators had their own turnstiles marked, in the time hon-oured way as "Sombra", "Sol" and "Sol y Sombra", (Shade, Sun and Sun & Shade,) the most expensive seats being in the shade as one would expect in a town where temperatures during the summer bullfighting season reach the high 30°Cs. Around the walled entrance enclosure where the bulls, and the horses if it is "Rejoneo", or bullfighting on horseback, wait to go into the intimate circle of life and death, there was a storage shed, a small cottage, unoccupied, and the infirmary. Here injured matadors, usually gored in the chest or the groin, would be carried by the other glitteringly-dressed participants in the ritual of La Corrida. I left the horses happily eating, apparently oblivious to the more ominous undertones of their glamorous quarters. Opening the wooden doors from the "Plaza" to the backyard, the silhouette of a tall, blond, skinny man emerging from the infirmary made me jump. He was shouting at two dogs tripping him up on the doorstep and then he fired off a quick series of unintelligible phrases in my direction, full volume. I tried Spanish and then English, to no avail and began to realise he was speaking to me in German - and was entirely stocious drunk at eight o'clock in the morning. Behind him I could glimpse the old fashioned medical set-up of the infirmary, various metal devices of torture and a shiny iron stretcher-bed where he had apparently slept. After quite a lot more one-sided "conversation" during which both his dogs lifted their legs and peed copiously on the remaining hay bales and sack of oats, he set about leaving. Up until then I had imagined he was a down-and-out who'd moved in for a night but, as the older dog settled down to wait for him in the yard, he left with his terrier, extracting a key like mine to the bull ring and I realised this was his home. I said farewell to the fussy old lady of my imagination.

Call me slow on the uptake but it wasn't until I was half-way to the local cafe for breakfast that I realised what had happened to my bottle of whiskey.

I wandered back through Cazorla town, filled with prosperous-looking people here for the Easter celebrations. Whole families, including a great many dogs on fancy leads with fancy jackets, paraded around the shops and squares and cafes. This was definitely a cut above anywhere I had stayed up to now and

I felt my best jeans and shirt (best of two that is) did not quite come up to scratch.

Penelope had sartorial problems in Cazorla too.

"Thought I would look as chic as possible when I went out shopping (Cazorla being a big pueblo of 12000 inhabitants) so I wore the smarter of my two jerseys with my Terylene skirt and black stockings. Soon realised that I was the subject of ridicule because of the latter: Only old women wear them in these parts. I went and bought some nylons."

Back outside the "Parador de la Estrella", the grandly named "posada" where Penelope stayed, I found the great wooden doors locked. Luckily there was a huge keyhole through which I could see a big bright room with shafts of sunlight and dust motes floating. Beyond was a sloping ramp leading down to the stables where, that winter day in 1961, there were fifteen horses, ponies and mules stabled. There were also two huge pigs to whom Penelope gave Marie biscuits when she was grooming her mare, saddened to think they would soon go the way of the pigs in Tiscar. They nosed her lovingly, unaware that in a day or two their piggy intestines would be hanging from the rafters full of black pudding. As I swapped eyes back and forth at the keyhole it looked to me as if the interior had not been disturbed for many years. Covered in smooth white dust were tables and chairs, plates and glasses, a donkey harness, a wooden stool, an iron pot hanging over the dead grate and a pair of calico leg wraps on the back of a chair. There were ropes and buckets and a lone shovel leaning against the wall, all silent and immobile, illuminated through the window by the morning sun from a busy street. This was Penelope's "Ritz" of a posada, with panes in all the windows and a bathroom on the second floor.

"...with a WC that really worked and didn't stink. Fortunately only cold water came out of the hot and cold bath taps so I was not tempted to have a bath. I did not want to wash the natural oil out of my skin...I would be certain to die at the next draughty posada I lodged in."

The smart new bedroom wing had been re-built in 1960 for French tourists who, even then, according to Penelope *"..flock here every summer (though how they have the nerve after what their grandfathers did to the best church, I don't know)."*

Gazing up at the second floor of this impressive building, I could see the window was, alas, now missing some panes of glass and wondered if that miraculous bathroom was still there. Overall this little dead-end alley leading to the old inn felt like a science fiction time machine. Out here it was Easter Week Cazorla 2019, yet if only I had the key to open this great door, I would be transported back to a November day in 1961.

Her landlord, Francisco Diez, was doing well. As well as his Parador de la Estrella, which earned him a good income year round, he also had an everything shop, opening onto the main Plaza where the Town Hall was. Here he sold animal feed, ironmongery, boots and shoes, clothes and, according to Don Juan Antonio Bueno, local historian, a wonderful selection of knives from Toledo and Albaicete where the best steel came from, the most memorable merchandise in the shop for a young lad.

I met Don Juan Antonio in the local library, a most charming and knowledgeable elderly professor, dressed accordingly in suit and tie. I noticed how very white his shirt was and how well-cared-for his hands. I felt embarrassed in his presence that my shirt looked as if it had been rejected by the tinkers and I kept my hands, still somewhat decorated by chorizo finger, firmly under the table throughout our interview. His explanation of Cazorla's history began in Roman times so we worked our way through a lot of kings and castles until we came to the era that was relevant to Messrs. Chetwode and Considine! He remembered Francisco Diez, who had, as Penelope mentions, a withered arm.

"He was very amusing, an animated talker. I was always popping in and out of the shop to see the knives and he also sold empty pig guts that people could buy and stuff themselves to make different kinds of sausages. He had his own olives outside town and made oil to be sold in the shop too. For his time he was a very forward thinker and a good businessman."

However, as Don Juan Antonio pointed out, this meant he was very ambitious for his sons, one went away to study and became a doctor and the younger, Manuel, was studying engineering when, in 1961, the English lady visitor helped him with his English which was considered vital even then. She quotes verbatim an hilarious extract from his English course book which starts:

"The English at Work: Ploughing. Look at this photograph (a very bad one indeed) Perhaps you are surprised to see a girl, she is English (and wearing a felt hat), driving a heavy tractor?"

It seems sad that the Diez family's efforts to educate their sons really guaranteed that they would go away. It must have happened as much here as in the smaller villages, this exodus of youth and talent. There were twelve thousand inhabitants of Cazorla in 1961 and now there are about eight thousand. Let's face it, an engineer and a doctor would not come back to run the family posada, however much like the Ritz it was. And what of Francisco´s olive groves and the highly successful shop that is no more?

"The olive groves were inherited sideways, to cousins. They shut the shop when they became too old and the posada continued for a few years more and then it closed. By the 1970´s farm animals were becoming less welcome in the middle of town and this caused difficulties for the "posadas" .

Cazorla seems to be a thriving centre now and even in 1961 there were French tourist coming here?

"The biggest change of all came to this town when the Sierra de Cazorla was proclaimed a National Park of Hunting in 1960. This brought an upper-class tourist boom, of which select visitors Franco was a part, with his hunting lodge, now the Parador. Later, in 1982 it was declared a Natural Park and that brought an influx of more ordinary tourists and a massive economic boost for Cazorla. The fame of the park was already spread by Felix Rodriguez de la Fuente, the first of his kind of naturalist in Spain. His hugely popular TV series in the 70´and the 80´s had everyone glued to the screen and, as soon as there was access, people just couldn´t wait to see it for themselves."

You can count me into that category!

"So we get plenty of tourists though there is still a certain amount of depopulation, not due to emigration but to the birth rate which has crashed to an average of 1.3 babies per couple."

I asked Don Juan Antonio about the olive groves lapping the town from the west like a sage-green tide on a shingly beach overlooked by cliffs that are the mountains.

"When olives first started encroaching on the cereal crops, there was still work for all, tilling, pruning, harvesting by hand;

but when Spain joined the EU and urgency for quantity and speed brought in the machinery that is now used throughout, it left many men out of work, and so it unfortunately continues. However less so in Cazorla than in other towns and villages because we have our Golden Goose, the Parque Natural de la Sierra de Cazorla Segura y las Villas."

Out on the streets again and the sun had disappeared into a strange murk, with sudden threatening gusts of wind banging doors and bending the trees in the square. I had been demented watching the weather forecast over the last twenty-four hours. There was rain forecast and the heaviest rain of all appeared to be due in three days' time which was when we were due to set off across the shelter-less (unless you count several million waist high olive trees) prairie to the west for the Sierra Magina.

Still, no time to worry for the moment as I had a visit awaiting me. Unlike Penelope, who relied on Poste Restante letters in various villages for news from home, my friends and neighbours were just a drive away. While hers could only sit in London or Berkshire and wonder how that crazy woman was faring in the wild lands of Andalusia, mine just had to jump in the car for four or five hours to come and see. Ian Baillie, with a Scots accent you could cut with a knife and a gammy leg, was immediately recognisable for his lurching stride and unquenchable spirit. He has walked the hills and valleys of Ireland where he and his family lived for thirty something years (and absolutely no impression was made on his Glasgow accent) and then transferred to Spain where he continues scaling tracks and trails. He has approached Santiago de Compostela from every known "camino" or pathway. He and I have a long history of pathfinding together and his lovely serene Norwegian wife, Aude, who does have an Irish accent, is the perfect foil for his dry humour. They were waiting for me in the main square in town across from Penelope´s "posada" as the Easter parades got going. We soon gave up trying to converse against the trumpets and drums, the slow marchers and the shrieking children racing and blowing whistles as the saint was born solemnly through the streets. Every time he passed his "home" church, where he will return for another year after this, he was given a little jig on his "costeleros" or bearers´ shoulders, a weird, cavorting, sacred figure. So very different to anything one would ever see in the English Protestant tradition of Penelope´s husband John Betjeman. Not for the first time it seemed extraordinary to me the fervour with which she had latched onto Roman Catholicism which she writes about in every chapter of her book, coming as she did from the quieter, simpler traditions of the Anglican Church.

Having already sampled the delicious trout from the mountain streams of the sierra, I was able to recommend them to Ian and Aude at dinner while branching out myself to a local speciality: black pudding mousse, served with hot toast and blackcurrent jam on the side. It is about one hundred times more delicious than it sounds. Food for the Gods, Penelope´s or any others.

April 18th

A poet, a painter and two good friends

I woke to the inevitable sound of pouring rain. The view from my window was eclipsed by a sheet of falling water off the roof; it was similar to being on the underside of Iguazu falls. Andalusia never does things by halves.

Very foolishly, considering I had spent the last two days frantically plugged in to the weather forecast which had predicted this, I had left my waterproofs with the horses so was entirely drenched during the ten-minute uphill charge to get to them. I then discovered how quickly a bullring can turn into a swimming pool, the horses up to their knees in water standing forlornly in the shallows round the edge as the tide rose. On the far side was a sloping, arched entrance down from the street, the only covered area where they would be safely enclosed within the bullring confines. We paddled (no of course I didn´t bring my wellies) over there and I managed to get their feed to them on the higher drier ground though it involved crossing a rushing stream where the concrete began. Walking back between the seating in the amphitheatre above the arena, I managed to avoid wading and for the next few days this is how I approached the animals in their chilly little porch. I don´t think Bruma left the shelter at all during the rainy weather, though Luqa ventured out to splash about a bit, probably hoping for rescue from this crazy adventure.

By this time I was sodden inside and out, streelish hair befitting a banshee and stuck all over with hay. Living in a hotel meant I had to make an effort to be halfway presentable, in particular when I flitted through reception, so I hosed myself down in the little yard where the bulls wait. I couldn´t have been more waterlogged anyway and at least I no longer looked like a porcupine. I had foolishly washed my spare clothes yesterday and, although dangled about my hotel room, they were not drying, so I had nothing else to put on. I sat around in my knickers for a bit eating a floppy version of French toast I had bought at the bakers as I was in no state to go down to the cosy bar for a coffee which I longed for. God love them, Ian and Aude came to the rescue with Aude´s dry clothes for me so I was able to emerge from my purdah and set off with them to Quesada as planned.

Quesada is a hilltop town, halfway between Tiscar and Cazorla, not a simple place to reach for me and the horses in 2019 without riding on the main road. Penelope made it quite easily from Tiscar as the road was still gravel and the traffic minimal. On arrival she installed La Marquesa in the "posada" and, as usual, went off to find the parish priest, much as I tended to seek out the mayor of each village who have now taken the place of the priest in knowing everyone and their business and answering questions asked by nosy foreign women. It was here that Penelope met two appealing Don Antonios. Firstly the priest who immediately took her under his wing:

"An exceptionally charming man...wreathed in smiles and busy receiving an endless stream of parishioners... I asked him to tell me the story of the Virgin of Tiscar. He welcomed me most warmly to his "pueblo" , invited me to luncheon, promised to tell me the story afterwards and in the meantime insisted on taking me to the town hall to meet the "Alcalde" (mayor), Don Antonio Navarrete, who is a nature poet of distinction."

In the office of the Culture Counsellor, Juan Antonio Lopez, I found a photograph of both the Antonios surrounded by cheerful students in the dress of the traditional "Tuna" band carrying every kind of instrument including mandolins. These bands began in the 12th century as a way for students to pay their tuition by serenading the public. It looks wintry and they are all wrapped up. Father Antonio is sporting a velvet-collared coat and a big grin behind his gold rimmed specs and poet Antonio, a broad handsome man in a thick overcoat, crouching forward for the photo to the level of one of the boy musicians who is posed down on one knee.

Only a year before Penelope's visit, Don Antonio Navarrete's close friend, the painter Rafael Zabaleta, had died at the young age of fifty-two. The poet was still broken-hearted at this loss and had buried his friend in the centre of the village cemetery and planted an almond tree above so that Rafael would have the blossom every spring. He also founded the first Rafael Zabaleta art gallery. Both of these men have since become famous in the world of Spanish literature and painting but they were not yet well known in 1961 and Penelope, having also found an unexpected depth of theological knowledge and argument in the parish priest, commented;

"I was deeply moved to find this nest of culture in such a remote mountain fastness: the theologian, the painter and the poet."

She and Father Antonio had some theological discussions on such subjects as infallibility which surely means that, in the brief two weeks of her journey, her comprehension and fluency in the Spanish language had improved immensely. On her preliminary guided tour across the mountains of Malaga province which she undertook with friends, the gypsy guide, Pitirri, had taught her how to say her Hail Marys in Spanish and few vital words to do with the care, shoeing and feeding of horses. She would write out these words to be learnt while riding along.

"By the time I set out on my own tour, therefore, I was equipped with a good set of nouns such as barley, straw, girth, crupper, saddle, horseshoe, blacksmith, but not more than six past participles: I have come, I have been, I have seen, I have suckled, I have read, I have eaten. ...

Suckled?

"Plunged into the heart of rural Andalusia I gauged my progress by the sermons I heard. The first one, delivered in Churriana in early October, was wholly incomprehensible, but by the end of November, after being on my own for a month, I could understand and enjoy the excellent preaching which is a great feature of Spanish church life – sermons of evangelical length lasting from thirty to forty minutes."

Forty minutes? Jesus, Joseph and Mary!

She also worked on a splendid spiel to explain herself as she arrived nightly in different "posadas". This started along the lines of *"I am English, I am on a tour of these mountains"* and went on with an early mention of her friend the Duke of

Wellington and that her horse belonged to him. She would then list all the places she had seen so far in Spain by which time, hopefully, her bedroom was ready for her and she could escape politely to write her journal and unpack. To begin with she sought to leave no pauses where her listeners might ask questions which she could not understand. On a couple of occasions, in desperation, she got onto fox-hunting which she thought would be of interest to the other "posada" folk, owners of mules and horses. Unfortunately, her Spanish was not up to explaining why the foxes were not hunted for their skins and the hounds were allowed to destroy them – a bewildering concept to the Andalusian audience.

The Story of the Virgin of Tiscar

More or less as recounted to Penelope Chetwode by Father Don Antonio, Parish Priest of Quesada 1961

St. Isicio, a disciple of St. Peter, brought the image of the Virgin of Tiscar to the mountains in the first century AD. A huge fuss was made of her and she became a symbol of her village.

In the 8th century, when the Moors conquered Tiscar, they took the image of the Virgin and held her in the prison where the sanctuary now stands, thinking she could make a useful hostage.

In 1319, the forces of the Archbishop of Toledo and Prince Don Pedro of Castile marched on Tiscar and the governor of the fortress, Mohammed Handoun, tried to destroy the Virgin by throwing her into the rushing water in the Cueva del Agua. But she kept rising up unharmed until he struck the head of the image with his sword and she sank. The Prince and the

Archbishop were told about this by a Muslim captive and raced to the cave at which point the Virgin bobbed up again with only the gash on her forehead, evidence of the disaster that had befallen her.

They took her to the church they were building on the site of the prison and there she stayed until the Archbishop decided to take her to Toledo. Turning out to be quite a stubborn wench, the Virgin of Tiscar slipped off the horse she was tied to and turned up again back in the church. They took the hint that she did not want to move house and there she stayed until 1936 when the "Reds" hammered her to pieces and then threw her once again into the depths of the Cueva del Agua. (Everywhere I went there were stories of the Republicans during the Civil War smashing sacred images into little pieces. It must have been quite time-consuming. Perhaps they would have been better employed for their cause if they had left God's stuff alone and concentrated on Franco's lot.)

In 1939, the sculptor Hinqueras made a new image using photographs and she was put back in her preferred home, the Sanctuary church in Tiscar. Three years later the scar on her forehead reappeared, exactly where the Moorish lord had speared her with his sword six hundred years previously.

Strangely, in spite of being something of a homebody, she doesn't seem to mind leaving her sanctuary every May to be carried the fourteen kilometres to Quesada where she stays all summer, returning for her birthday on 8th September. I think the rose petals they shower her with from the balconies of Quesada might swing the balance. A pretty spectacular welcome after all.

I, also, felt that this village had more than its share of talent. In Juan Antonio Lopez´ office in the Town Hall there were many magazines containing poetry, stories and articles, all by the contemporary folk of Quesada and all of a high quality. Antonio Navarrete, who was a very popular mayor of Quesada during many years, claimed he was a disciple of another famous poet honoured in this town, Antonio Machado.

Parking Ian and Aude´s car as close to the Zabaleta art gallery as we could, we splashed through the puddles, huddled under an umbrella, and climbed the slippery marble steps into the ultra-modern building. I could tell this wasn´t Ian´s bag, and galleries and museums aren´t mine really but I told myself it was all in the name of research.

However, as soon as I walked into the first room and saw those colours and characters and vibrant life framed in front of me, I was hooked. Vivid faces looked out of his canvases, the same faces I had been seeing all around me during the previous two weeks. Generous, solid, country faces, open and almost innocent, with practical hands laid resting in their lap or gripped around some farm implement. Some of his paintings are simple self-portraits or of one figure alone, some are crowded with so many people and events they barely fit on the canvas. Nearly all of them look at you from their frames with the straightforward serene brown eyes that welcomed me at every stop along the way on my pilgrimage across Granada and Jaen provinces. His countryside is instantly recognisable – the tilt of the hills, the lie of the steep fields and the geometry of the stones in the walls. There are more animals and the enclosures are colourful with varied crops, but it is unquestionably here in these mountains.

Zabaleta wrote of his work: "What you will see straight away is my love for this corner of my land, for this village of

Quesada that has always been faithful in all places and in all circumstances."

They had to drag me out into the rain so we could go and have lunch in a bar just across from what was once the posada, which the Marquesa found smellier than most as the bedding they used was household refuse. Now it is just a tall house with a big door.

In January 2007, nearly fifty years after the death of his dear friend the artist, Don Antonio Navarrete died of heart failure aged 80. I climbed up to the cemetery behind the town to see where he was laid to rest near Zabaleta, under the soft green foliage and spring blossom of the huge almond tree. In one of his poems called "Reflection in Autumn" which seems to me to be about shedding this mortal coil, Navarrete wrote;

"When the leaves fly, we must leave, definitely.

If the time has come to return, it is not possible to delay so much beauty

Of autumn rains on branches and stones, nor the tiredness of the sun, velvet

In the clear memory of the eyes. Because it would be selfishness,

A dark greed, retaining the excitement we have left,

When new eyes, other eyes, need the gold of life…"

Our return drive to Cazorla took a lot less than Penelope's ride there and we didn't have to slither down beside the Castillo de la Yedra, but I think we were just as damp as she was when we got back. The rain continued to pour and the horses to cower in their bullring porch. I squelched around in Aude's clothes on the principle that while I got them saturated I could be trying to get mine reasonably dry. With this in mind all my dripping garments and sodden shoes went back to my long suffering friends´ rented apartment where there was more possibility of drying things. Aude even hairdryer-ed my revolting trainers which was entirely beyond the call of duty. If I was organising the Easter processions, you lovely woman, you would be right up there on the "costeleros" shoulders leading the saints.

Tonight we walked upstream from our end of town along a landscaped path beside the Rio Cerezuelo, leaving it to plunge into its tunnel under the Plaza Santa Maria while we went above ground to have supper in one of the restaurants beside the roofless church. Snails and mushrooms featured largely on menu boards outside every eating place, both of which appear like magic as soon as the ground gets wet. My "bacalao" or salt-ed cod with wild mushrooms was so good I was almost glad it was raining...almost.

*

April 19th

Plentiful waters

The showman and the saint left me this morning, disappearing into the drizzle with a lot of cracks about "Irish weather" (the showman) and requested reassurances that I would not catch pneumonia and would mind myself (the saint). They left me with "clothes to get wet in" giving me more possibility of riding out dry when I left on the next leg.

I had to take the decision that, in view of the dire forecast for the morrow, I would not set out as planned to start to cross the wide, rolling, exposed plain until the day after. I started to ring the various stopping places that were expecting my little party, to rearrange things. The hotel in Jodar I had to cancel altogether, on Easter weekend. It had been booked since February. I offered to pay anyway.

"No problem, no problem, Karen. We are really sorry not to see you but of course you can´t ride in this. Take care with your horses," and this is someone I had never even met.

With a whole day in hand before my next helpers arrived, I went to early mass at the church across the square from Penelope´s "posada" where she had attended under the gaze of curious local children. Sure enough at least two of the multiple dogs I had seen in the town had also come to worship. One sat solemnly in the aisle, concentrating on the service but the one in pew in front of me, a small white person with a fancy hairdo and muddy paws turned his back on the Holy Sacrament and studied me throughout. Strange human, wrong smell, odd clothes…

Having seen to things of the spirit, I decided to concentrate on the practical and try and find the best way out of the town for us in two days' time, Easter Sunday. I found a street on the other side of the Rio Cerezuelo that went deep into the old town and then swung round taking me in the right direction. Unfortunately what appeared to be a splendid dirt track on the map leading off this lane, turned out to be vertical concrete. This is indeed the curse of modern Andalusia. Whenever there is a crisis (pronounced "creesees" and always financial) and people are out of work, the Junta de Andalusia sets them all to "improving communications" as they call it. There can't be a single Andalusian countryman who doesn't know how to lay concrete. This path made no nod whatsoever to the art of zig-zag: all that could possibly climb up the horrendous ski run would be a car, or possibly a motorbike, in first gear and high revs. Nor had they left even half a metre of verge so it was really impassable to four legs. I scrambled up bent double as I knew our way was either this or the main road which would add four kilometres at least. At the crest of the rise the track turned to dirt again and had a name "Antiguo Camino de Cazorla", or the Old Way of Cazorla, with views in every direction. I passed an old "cortijo", newly roofed and sitting beside a pounding, hot-chocolate-brown stream tearing downhill. It was a little flavour of how things used to be before the era of the OLIVE. Two cats sat on a pile of straw at the big wooden entrance door and, although I could not see into the courtyard, I could hear contented hens clucking and goat bells and enjoy a faint whiff of farmyard.

I decided to return through the gentler olive groves, scraping the platform soles of mud off my shoes every few strides. This was the way we would have to climb up on Sunday, and I knew my prayers that morning would be mainly about horse shoes staying on for just a little bit longer, please God. I had a spare "boot" to replace a missing shoe but that would only last three strides in this clinging wet clay. After every stoop for mud scraping, I straightened up and gaped at the theatrical panorama of Cazorla and its sierra, clarified and magnified by the intermittent rain and limpid moist air. Two very smiley men in a four-wheel drive passed me and stopped to ask if I was the owner of the horses they had seen in the bullring. They were dressed from head to toe in baggy white coveralls and wore face masks pushed up on the top of their heads. We bemoaned the weather that stopped us from getting on with things. In my innocence I thought these friendly beekeepers could probably not work with their hives and smokers in the rain. However, half an hour later, I saw them in a grove unloading any number of canisters and spray guns and realised they were not bee keepers after all, but potential killers of bees and any other insects who came in their way. The use of pesticides is not new of course: Penelope met a middle-aged man with a deep soothing voice in one of her "posadas" who was travelling round on a motor scooter advising farmers which sprays to use against which pests. Much as she felt she wanted to attack chemical farming, she blamed mental and physical sloth after eight hours in the saddle plus her inability to conjure up phrases such as "organic manure" or "balance of nature" in Spanish for not taking him on. I had no such excuse for not stopping and having a discussion with these two fellas but – the mud was deep, the rain was wet and, well, they were so friendly and concerned for my horses in the flooded bullring, it would have been downright churlish!

All along my way, springs and streams, troughs and wells gushed with mountain water, each with its resident nightingale, the harder it rained the louder they sang. Perhaps because it is such a precious commodity and at many times of year so scarce, water holds an important place in the hearts of Andalusians. Spurning the town water from the tap, family members regularly drive with big plastic containers or walk with their mules and "cantaros" to outlying springs where the water is known to be good water - "buena agua". Near where I live are the springs of Hedionda, famously reputed to have cured Julius Caesar of herpes. These natural hot waters emerge in a spherical vault built into the ground, originally Roman and remodelled in Moorish times, and then run across a 16th century aqueduct to various pools. Summer and winter the locals come to the hidden glade to reap the benefits of the "good water". One elderly gentleman from my village regularly walks and hitches the 24kms there and back to bathe and keep his psoriasis at bay. By one of my horses´ fields, a little trickle in the summer which turns into a gushing spout from the rock after rain is reputed to be good for eyes, both for bathing them and drinking. In Huelago, Granada, there was great rejoicing when, in 2010, the "Miracle Spring" started to run again after disappearing for twenty-eight years. This water cures spots and eczema and boils and all sorts of skin problems. People come from miles away to bathe in it and take litres of it home to continue the treatment. Rather surprisingly, considering its reputation for aridity, Jaen province has the most springs of fresh water in all of Andalusia, over three-thousand, compared with, for example, Cordoba, which has under a thousand. At a trough under a spring in the Cazorla Natural Park, a woman stood aside to let my horses drink and then continued filling the ten glass bottles with rubber stoppers she was loading into her jeep. This water, she told me, strengthens the heart and makes you feel full of life.

While I was foostering around killing time in the rain, my old car was belting north towards me with two of my most intrepid friends on board.

"How can we help?" they had unwisely asked.

HAH! I knew exactly how.

Nikki, long-time friend from England, mother of my godson Joe, is 6ft of blond, fit, lean woman and, best of all on this occasion, an experienced camper, Scout leader, and outdoor expert. I had decided to ride direct from Cazorla to Jodar and realised it would take two days and there was nothing, but nothing, in between. No villages with bars, no old "cortijos" to shelter in, no "casas rurales" to welcome us, so the only alternative was camping. Who better to be in charge of that than Nikki?

With her came Marcela whom I had not seen since our first tentative exploration here back in November. Marcela is always up for anything, funny and practical and the sort of person who makes a trip a party. Plus she was dying to see how I was getting on, so, three weeks ago when she was still in

Uruguay for the winter, I had left my car, laden with horse feed and camping gear, at her house and now the pair of them were about to arrive in Cazorla.

First I had to break the news to them that our ride had been postponed for a day and we were not setting out tomorrow. Then, after a nod to the historical, if rather damp, delights of the town we actually found an Irish bar and settled in for the evening. Marcela who, rather like Penelope, doesn't really drink unless forced by someone like me, had fizzy water. I couldn't believe it. Going to an Irish bar for fizzy water is rather like going to a prostitute for a hug - but everyone to their own. Nikki and I hit the gin and the Guinness on her behalf.

The only other thing I remember about the evening is that, no matter where we went, it was absolutely impossible to get that standby accompaniment to a glass of something, a little dish of olives. Barman after barman denied the existence of olives as a tapa, which, considering the million olive trees encroaching at the bottom of the street, struck us as absolutely hysterical.

*

April 20th

The golden city

My decision not to ride out from Cazorla today proved well-founded. The heavens opened and it bucketed down all day long. First, a squelchy visit with Marcela and Nikki to the bullring to visit the horses sequestered in their covered corner. We walked round the seating above the flood with bundles of hay and buckets of oats. (I had already hung "Do not disturb" on the bedroom we were sharing in case any long suffering hotel staff had a conniption on entering, and I had bought a box of chocolates for the poor cleaning lady when we left). Then my German neighbour emerged, a tad less inebriated than usual, and, with one glance at my glamorous friends, started to chat charmingly in both English and Spanish. Huh!

Marcela and I drove off in the car to deliver horse feed ahead of my ride and relieve the pressure on the vehicle's doors, ready to burst with the amount of stuff loaded in there. We managed to get the car stuck in slippy mud in Montejicar where a little pickaheen of a man called Fernando (grumpy but, I felt, with a heart of gold) had agreed to put up my horses in the land round his barn. Apart from that, our trip was long and uneventful…and wet. Occasionally, through the scudding clouds, we could see the city of Ubeda, draped along a distant ridge to the north.

I don´t think I could have believed then how different it would all be when I finally went there three months later.

*

Ubeda. Visited without the horses in July 2019

Penelope´s Holy Grail on her journey was Ubeda. She had been told of the many ancient churches and the beautiful architecture it held and this was something that she could not resist, her two passions, the Roman Catholic faith and History of Art coming together in such abundance in one place. Ubeda is a city and I soon realised, when I looked into it, that I was not going to be able to ride in on horseback and find somewhere for my transport to stay. The alternative, putting the horses up in some kind of field or barn a few kilometres away, meant that I would spend my time hiking back and forth. I could not leave the place out of my journey because it was such a key destination for our heroine so I decided to cheat and visit Ubeda by car after I had finished the ride.

Hot July, and friend Corky, wife of seven-league-legs Jon, and I drove for four hours across the baked countryside I had ridden over back in squelchy April, leaving the plain to climb onto the ridge to the north with the towns of Ubeda and Baeza decorating the top.

"Set in stone", golden stone, describes Ubeda perfectly.

The form and look of the old town cannot have changed since Penelope stayed here. Palaces, monuments, squares, churches, all perfectly proportioned, sitting side by side for eternity. Most of them raised to the glory of God, aristocracy and wealth on this long, narrow hill above the plain in the 14th and 15th centuries. Crowded together, leaving no gaps for modern construction and, even to the most corrupt of town planners, too obviously precious to be knocked down to make way for Penelope's most hated word - "progress" - they have survived unchanged. We drove in and reached the centre of town and our little hostel easily, dying to explore what we had already seen of the shady, cobbled streets.

Penelope did not have such an easy journey. From the beginning she went wrong on what was then a forty-six kilometre drive by the main road, though a lot less by mule path from Cazorla to Ubeda because:

"I made the most fatal mistake of my tour: I did not believe the directions of a muleteer. I thought I knew better....I was fed up with the metalled road. Away to the north I saw a track after my own heart and against my better judgement I let myself be lured towards it, riding boldly across country through deep plough."

She continued on the wrong trails, jumping up stone-faced banks, and looking for a bridge over the River Guadalquivir which she had had quite enough of by this time. She compared it out loud, unfavourably, with English rivers, whose green banks and clear water were so much more beautiful in her opinion.

"Only your name is romantic."

On and on she went, turning back on one occasion having mistakenly gone several kilometres out of her way.

"*I had to ride ... in the growing dusk with lorries flying past so I held out a white handkerchief in my left hand to avoid being run into from behind...*" (To think, after all her adventures, she had a handy handkerchief and it was still white says a lot about the organisational skills of a cavalry officer's daughter!) It was an exhausted, woebegone horse and rider who finally arrived at a gate in the city wall of Ubeda.

"*We entered Ubeda at the lower end, through the horseshoe arch of the Moorish gate of the Rosal. The poor Marquesa was so weary she tried to turn into one house after another, hoping it might be the "posada".*"

First she went to the Parador, which had been recommended to her, but was sad to find no stables. Joined by a young man who had done his military service with horses, they then tried another "posada" to no avail.

"*I was leading the Marquesa by this time and could hardly put one foot before another, nor could she, for having gone so much out of our way we could not have covered much less than sixty kilometres since leaving Cazorla. If only someone would provide us with a stable I would willingly have slept in a loft, or in a manger.... or on the cobbles beside the muleteers. We were now directed to a second "posada" but the landlord had no "paja"! (straw). I was too desperate to laugh. I turned to the young man and commanded: "Take me to the Guardia Civil". (Well, not THAT woebegone). So there we went and it seemed like a five kilometre walk right to the outskirts of town...I asked to see the Colonel and implored him to stable the poor Marquesa. He was very sympathetic but feared this was impossible and told me of yet a third posada...I began to curse the religious mania which had brought me here.*"

WOW!

From one of the many "miradores" or lookouts in this city on the ridge, gazing south across a myriad of olives which sixty years ago were the ploughed fields Penelope struggled through, we could see exactly how she had ridden the last part of the trail. Starting at the Rosal gate it was possible to follow the steep cobbled streets past the Parador and the various posadas she had tried to the Guardia Civil training barracks on the far side of town. It was indeed a long and tiring walk even for Corky and me, and we had done nothing in the way of a sixty-kilometre ride that morning. Thank goodness, the young man who was helping Penelope suggested that his father-in-law might have space behind his little house for the mare. As it turned out, the head of the household was not there but his three daughters, Trini and Pepita, with whom Penelope would share a bedroom, and Paqui, married to Mario the guardian angel, welcomed the Marquesa through the narrow door, across the cobbled hall and out into the tiny yard and stable at the back. It was already occupied by two ewes, three lambs, two very fat tame rabbits, seven hens, a collie with her pup and a black pony. It must have been a bit of a squash but here the tired horse lived for the four days they were in Ubeda, apparently peacefully, probably because the menagerie did not include any pigs which she was inclined to persecute with sneaky kicks.

Trying to find out more about the Esposito family who were so kind to our pilgrims, we made enquiries in the splendid Hospital de Santiago which is at the top of the avenue where the little house was. The nice man helping with the early morning cleaning turned out to be called Esposito as well, though we soon discovered there seemed to be a lot of them about. Strangely no one actually remembered our particular branch of the family though, and, apart from the really wonderful Dolores who was ninety something (she wasn't quite sure herself), nobody we found was old enough to have been around in 1961. However, as always, people couldn't have been more helpful and interested, just as Penelope describes her particular friends in Ubeda all those years ago.

In 2019 the treasures and delights of the city are undiminished and with 'Two Middle-Aged Ladies in Andalusia' clutched in my rather sweaty hand, we felt as if we had a special advantage over the few other tourists we saw who just had the official guidebook with them.

At the time that Penelope visited, some of the churches remained in a partially-destroyed condition having been sacked in the Civil War. In particular, the Pantheon of San Salvador, next door to the Parador was in a sorry state. She used to go and have "ritzy" breakfasts in this hostelry nearly every day because there was no movement towards morning refreshment where she was staying . As she put it:

"No one could accuse the Spaniards of being slaves to early morning cups of tea."

Her Parador breakfasts, which were a real treat, included:

"Russian tea, real toast, the first butter I have tasted since leaving Illora, peach jam and a delicious Ubeda variation on the Bath bun," (we found and tried those!) and from there she went next door into the church, built in the 16th century by the influential Cobos family, the same who were instrumental in the building of the Santa Maria Church in Cazorla, as a mausoleum. She found one side chapel had been used as a kitchen, fuelled by the carved statues from the rest of the church. The sacristy was emptied of its treasures and a small statue of St

John the Baptist, attributed to Michelangelo, hammered into fragments. However, when she tried to contribute some money towards the restoration work, the priest said there was no need because it was all being carried out entirely at the expense of the Duchess of Medinaceli. Rather along the lines of the billionaires who raced with their millions to restore Notre Dame after the fire in 2019, the very wealthy were vying even then to do important, well-publicised good deeds for the church. Doubtless hoping to go straight to heaven as a result. Well, I saw how far the good Duchess's contribution had gone and indeed it is a beautiful place once again. The extraordinary retablo was not to my taste, one can only cope with so much encrusted gold leaf, but the vertiginous swirly tiled floor might well lead to unplumbed depths or delights of the spirit and I nearly fell over backwards gazing at the ceiling, dizzying in glorious paintings high, high above the world of mere mortals. This was presumably out of reach of even the church gutting "Reds" as Penelope called them. As an example of the transcendental talents of early Spanish architects and stonemasons, San Salvador is unsurpassable, even though one irreverent professor a few hundred years later was heard to refer to the main entrance doorway as "A load of old gothic".

The Church of San Lorenzo, hard up against the south city walls above the endless, hazy Guadalquivir valley far below, was also damaged in the Civil War. The wide, inspiring interior is now being reborn as a centre for culture and art. Still with the pretty west gallery that Penelope mentions, and a lively coloured mudejar ceiling, but no longer housing the "andas", the chariots which carry the holy figures through the streets during religious festivals. In 1961 these were all stored in San Lorenzo wearing gingham covers to keep the dust off. Lifting the gingham to peer beneath, Penelope found a chariot of beaten silver upon which the Virgin of Guadeloupe is brought to Ubeda from her mountain chapel to spend the summer months in the city, rather as the Virgin of Tiscar goes to Quesada. Now, in what was once a desolate space, murals are being slowly and painstakingly revealed beneath the white-wash, and the stonework and floors restored. A rather startling exhibition of nude photography was on display in the sacristy and, even more unexpected, so was a glass case full of human skulls, found when they excavated the catacombs below. The team doing the renovations were intrigued by my book and, as often happened when I showed non-English speakers the paragraphs that might interest them, they fixated and misin-terpreted the one word or phrase they recognised. In this case they saw the name "Tarzan" which had apparently been the nickname of a famous local gypsy so they thought he must be written about on that page. I let them down as gently as I could, explaining that it was the name of the collie puppy where Penelope was staying.

I learnt two things in the Church of San Lorenzo. One was to cease immediately calling the thrones upon which the saints are carried through the streets "carrozas". I thought this referred to any kind of float or cart but it turns out to have roots in carnivals and fairgrounds and would cause shock and horror to the brotherhoods involved in the carrying of these sacred figures and who take it all very seriously. This was told me with a lot of laughter by the charming girl presiding over all the renovations. It was a man with a terrier on catacomb pest-control duty who explained why all the old churches have doors within doors. The huge high wooden entrance doors are opened only when the saints on their thrones are on the move or perhaps when someone very important is visiting. Otherwise only the little doors within them open and this is so that you jolly well have to get off your horse when attending mass as he won't fit through them!

In the magnificent church of Santa Maria, still a mosque in the 13th century and grown organically and pleasingly through all the architectural vagaries for the next six centuries, we found Our Lady of Guadeloupe. She sat in a bower of pink and white flowers in her own special chapel. Tiny, dainty and pretty as a picture in her pink and white and silver robe, she holds a crescent moon in her lap, symbol, I believe, of new birth and of silver itself. I lit several candles for her, aware that she would not have been travelling on her beaten silver "anda" to visit in damp, grey November 1961, so here was a little bit of holiness Penelope had not seen first!

We walked and walked among renaissance, mudejar, gothic and baroque architecture, in the narrow streets that gave us shade and the wide squares where breezes blew the peppery scent of olives up from the valleys. We found a tack shop in the old cobbled main street, attached to a toy shop and I bought a hoof pick as a souvenir, just in case it was the same place Penelope bought a leather wine "bota" for her husband John Betjeman. We went to see Saint John of the Cross, Carmelite friar, mystic and poet, his carved image lying peacefully in the oratory dedicated to him above the little cell where he died aged forty-nine in 1591. I only wanted to see the oratory but our tickets included a twelve-room museum. Now, I have a strange reaction to the word "museum", a yawn rises in my throat instantly and my shoes develop lead insoles. However, we went round this one, mainly because there did not seem to be any other way out once we had gone into the oratory. I´m glad we did. This humble man wrote wonderful lyrical poetry, which spoke, not only of God, but of the Spanish countryside he spent his life travelling through and in my tiny way I recognised his sentiments.

"My Beloved is the mountains,
The solitary wooded valleys,
The strange islands,
The roaring torrents,
The whisper of the amorous gales;
The tranquil night
At the approach of the dawn,
The silent music,
The murmuring solitude,
The supper which revives, and enkindles love."

I have a feeling that supper was Holy Communion though, and not my much-favoured "hamburguesa completa".

This saint´s lifework was forming a new order of more austere Carmelites, known as the "descalces" or Barefoot Carmelites. The old order of Carmelites were not pleased with this idea and the museum´s English version of the story had one wonderful Google Translate moment which Corky spotted.

"His excellent qualities of a formator of religious men and women made him to travel to Madrid. To Toledo, however, he was pushed by the furious distrust of the Footwear Carmelites, who confined him in a gloomy prison convent."

The Synagogue of Water was hidden under the city for nigh on seven hundred years until it was discovered by a developer at the beginning of the 21st century. It was excavated and opened to the public in 2007. The Sephardic Jews who had to flee in the 13th century left it ready for their return and so it remained beneath the busy streets, silently waiting. This is probably the most moving place of all in this city of Christian churches.

Corky and I had our last supper in Ubeda at a bar down by the Rosal gate and walked back to our hostel through the cooling streets at 11pm as the city came to life around us. We had an early start to drive home before the heat won next day.

Penelope describes her last feast with the Espinosa family in their little house where the whole family assembled in her honour and they killed the fatted rabbit for her, taken from La Marquesa's stable and sacrificed in the living room before her eyes. This, they explained, was so that everyone knew it was not a cat, which seemed to be something that she mentions more than once in her chapter about Ubeda, cat meat substituted for rabbit or hare. Come to think of it, although we saw plenty of dogs, I do not remember seeing one cat while we were there...

Once again the English lady visitor had problems with the Spanish glass-spouted "porron," pouring the wine up her nose this time, while aiming for her mouth. She wasn't a great drinker, Penelope, she needed more practice. I learnt that at my mother's knee, as they say!

On November 27th 1961, she and La Marquesa set forth to carry on their journey. Behind them they left the hospitable Esposito family and one lonely fat rabbit, parts of whose best friend were riding out through the Granada gate, leaving Ubeda forever.

*

Back in Cazorla, in April 2019, the evening rain seemed to be letting up a tiny bit, bringing us hope for the ride on the morrow, but we still laid every bit of waterproof clothing we possessed out in our hotel room and agreed that nobody else in Spain could be planning on spending Easter Day as we were. I secretly hoped that our route, which I had studied in advance, would not take us through any unnoticed waterways where we might well have to swim the horses across after the deluge.

From the top: Arriving at the Bullring. 'Girl with Still Life' by Artist Rafael Zabaleta Leaving Cazorla in the rain

*

April 21st

The Romans, the Iberians and a night under canvas

Leaving the box of chocolates and a note of apology for the hotel cleaner, we slipped out into a silent grey Easter morning of black lowering skies.

The cosy Hotel Puerto de Cazorla is worth a mention. In spite of my occupying a three bedded room for the first three nights on my own in Cazorla, they only charged me for an individual, in one of their busiest weeks of the year. They were always welcoming and put up with the inevitable debris I shed in my wake every day and, in the little bar restaurant and in reception, their big grins and interest carried me through the vagaries of the weather.

In fact, with very few exceptions, once I explained my journey to the people I met along the route, I received everything they had to offer in the way of support, practical advice and help. Many threw themselves into the adventure, dying to be part of it in some small way. The gorgeous lad who generously topped up my leather "bota" with wine as a surprise is a perfect example. It was indeed a surprise, as it was half full of whiskey already! I was very seldom allowed to pay anything for the horses' accommodation or feed when they provided it and, where the Mayor of the town or village was involved, I frequently found my own B&B expenses were covered too.

We packed up all the horse equipment in the bullring and loaded it into the car, the first time on my journey that the horses would not be carrying the pack. The great thing about having two helpers over the next couple of days was that one could ride along on the horse without a pack and the other drive, giving us car support along the way. Such luxury for me - no horse to lead, a companion to ride with and a picnic waiting at our halfway point.

Walking alongside the horses to begin with we navigated through the narrow alleys of Cazorla, only an occasional "señora" to be seen out scrubbing her front step in preparation for the day that was in it. Half way through the maze of alleyways we drew into a doorway to let a bicycle past and Bruma lifted her tail and deposited the most enormous steaming heap on that doorstep. We slunk away at speed and I couldn't help imagining the face of the lady who would shortly open her door, scrubbing brush and mop at the ready, to find that unexpected Easter egg waiting for her - in a town with no farm animals at all. Stopping to water the horses at the magnificent trough in the deserted Plaza Santa Maria, who should come merrily staggering up to us, talking German today, but the other occupant of the bullring? He was apparently sad to see us go, as was his terrier who fondly lifted his leg on mine as a sign of affectionate farewell. Once out of the town, Marcela and I mounted up in our voluminous rain capes leaving Nikki to return the bullring key to the "Policia" and follow along on roads in the laden car.

After days of hanging around it was wonderful to be on the move again, even in murky drizzle and muddy olive groves. Compared to the two ranges of mountains, the Sierra de Cazorla and the Sierra Magina, that border it to the west and east, the land we were to ride across looks like flat "campo" from a distance. However it turned out to be undulating with quite steep hills every few kilometres and the route I had picked out for us mainly followed the higher ground. Whenever we descended into the lower olive groves the horses slid and slithered down, the wet clay building up on their hoofs into incredibly sticky stilts, so our progress was slow.

Just to the south of us, on a small rise in the ground, hidden today in the misty drizzle, was the site of the Roman villa of Bruñel. Dating from the 2nd century AD it was occupied well into the 4th century and contained a fine "peristyle" or continuous portico with an atrium and bathing pool. There are apparently some very interesting mosaics and a bust of Thetis with crab's legs. When I tried to check this extraordinary fact online, all I got were people trying to sell me crabs legs to eat, so I have to take the information at face value. The villa was burnt to the ground in the 5th century and is only partly excavated to this day, five hundred square metres uncovered and, it is believed, another fifteen hundred still waiting to be investigated containing many more treasures, possibly with crustaceous legs? On a bright sunny Sunday with dry ground under our hoofs we would certainly have made the couple of kilometres detour to go and have a look but our journey was already complicated by the conditions of the day and the idea of hanging around to look at anything in the downpour seemed unthinkable; quite apart from the machinations involved in obtaining the key from the "Policia Local" in Quesada.

Another twelve or so kilometres along our trail to the north, between us and the agricultural town of Peal de Becerro, is the Royal Tomb of Toya. The story goes that a villager was working the land in 1909 when he uncovered some enormous stones which turned out to be the entrance to the two thousand three hundred year old grave of a rich Iberian aristocrat. The cave was full of goodies, including the wheels of a war chariot and some beautiful kraters, decorated vessels for diluting wine with water. First I ever heard of them - can't be many in our ancient sites in Ireland. The Royal Tomb of Toya is the finest example of Iberian burial architecture in the country. Penelope had heard of this funeral chamber and had thought of visiting but, like us, decided against it due to inclement weather and the several kilometre detour involved. For her, riding to Ubeda, it was well south of her trajectory; for us, too far to the north. There is another similar tomb near Hornos de Peal where we hoped to camp the night, but that is inaccessible to visitors.

It seems that ancient peoples, such as the Romans and the Iberians, favoured the fertile flat lands for their important set-tlements, rather than the inhospitable mountains crenellating the horizon.

We were heading west and Penelope had been riding north but it was in this terrain, then cultivated for cereal crops, that she had become very lost in the rain, going far out of her way, so I was very careful to stick to our planned route even if it was tricky. In spite of the claggy complications it was a beautiful ride. There is a lot of talk of the herbicides used in the olive groves and there was a very-easily-seen divide between those who did and those who didn't. Some groves were completely bare of vegetation, or had circles of bald ground right under each tree and greenery everywhere else. However, more than half the land we passed today was obviously untouched by chemicals with lush grass and banks of wild flowers like impressionist water colours in the gentle drizzle. Undeterred by the moist atmosphere, butterflies were enjoying the blooms and blossom, mainly swallowtails and tiny blue fellas that the Spanish call "Little Cupids". The grass was opulently abundant as far as two Andalusian horses were concerned and Luqa and Bruma were allowed lots of extra elevenses on the banks of the many happy streams while Marcela sang Uruguayan folk songs to us. It was a wonderful treat for them after their long penance in the concrete porch of the flooded bullring. I recorded the birdsong on my phone as they grazed, a cacophony of delighted tweets and trills, hoots and whistles, "rain, glorious rain and still more to come", with the rhythmic chumping of the horses and the pitter-patter of the raindrops on my waterproof cape as a background beat.

Nikki met us with a picnic where a minor road crossed our "cañada". We didn't dare take the car far off the road, remembering how we had got mired yesterday, but it was lovely to sit on a rock eating and drinking with the horses tied to the olive trees and all extraneous equipment safely stowed in the car.

My idea for a walking trail called "La Ruta de Penelope" might be somewhat challenging if participants had to cross this way as there is absolutely nowhere for them to shelter or eat, but I planned that they would follow the route of Messrs Chetwode and Marquesa via Ubeda so this should not be a problem; plenty of refreshment and shelter for walkers, if not horses, in the city and manageable distances for people on foot. On the other hand, mountain bikers would love crossing the plain east to west like we did, though probably in the dry season. They could do it in a day, our two-day ride came to nigh on fifty kilometres, nothing for the bikes, though there were some unexpectedly long and steep climbs.

After lunch we ascended out of the olives, up and up to the top of a long escarpment overlooking the stretch of cultivated groves at our feet, serried ranks and geometric patterns as far as the eye could see. The going was less sticky and the rain lessened and I felt glad that, unwittingly, I had brought us to a lighter, brighter vantage point on my pre-planned map. As we looked back to the Sierra de Cazorla, engulfed in black cloud, and far ahead to the Sierra Magina, also stormy and dark, the sky cleared above us and the rain stopped. There was a Moorish watchtower in the foreground, and beyond, on the northern horizon, was Penelope´s ultimate destination, Ubeda, draped like white lace, also in a patch of sunlight. We were silenced by the emptiness and the peace of it all.

Another muddy stream to cross in the valley, scents of wild mint and honeysuckle, and we came to our destination for the night. Scout Leader Nikki had set up camp for us, weirdly under the enormous metal awning of a huge, locked machinery shed. I had been aware that this place existed because it belonged to a friend of Jose Coronado in Hinojares called Victor, but it would have been needle-in-a-haystack stuff trying to find one machinery shed in all those thousands and thousands of hectares of olives, if not for technology. He sent us a location online which Nikki followed and there she was, my grubby old car safely parked and a heap of fairly dry firewood ready to light for our camp fire. Once the horses were tethered on some grass the colour of an Emerald Isle postcard, we wandered a couple of kilometres to a hamlet called Hornos de Peal, or Ovens of Peal. Maybe because the original cereal crops here meant that there was a whole village of bakers, or maybe, and I think more likely, it refers to kilns for brick-making. Nothing at all happens here now. It is hard to describe the completely pointless feeling the little place engenders, partly because it is dropped like a discarded white handkerchief on the plain with no real reason to be where it is. We met a man with a loaf of bread and a yoghurt who told us that there used to be fifteen hundred people and animals when the fields were full of crops, and now there are forty souls and no beasts. The bar has closed, the shop has closed and his bread came from Peal de Becerro. The church, firmly bolted and padlocked, bore the stone crests of some noble family and there was a handsome walled "cortijo", the big house of the village, drowned in lilac and banksia rose, which they call "rosa picanin" here. But the gates were barred and overgrown and there was a real feeling of abandonment - more than anywhere I had been so far. Really desolate. Only the perfume after the rain of dog roses and rampant lilac bushes run wild brought a little comfort to the abandoned houses in various states of disrepair.

Although one might expect the depopulation to be worse in Andalusia, Spain´s acknowledged poorest area, further north, particularly in the great blank central provinces of Aragon and Castilla La Mancha , the problem is more severe. On my trek I was seeing villages with fewer inhabitants than fifty years ago and empty houses but in areas such as Los Montes Universales between Guadalajara and Cuenca, the settlements are completely deserted, houses crumbling and going back to nature. Unbelievably, there are areas where the population is now sparser than Siberia, calculated at 1.7 people per square kilometre. In Castilla y Leon, near Soria, one of the problems was Franco's decision to plant twenty-two thousand hectares of prime cereal farming land with pine trees for paper, leaving local farmers with nothing to farm. Pine trees do not give work as olives do, though even in this industry, the EEC tactic of encouraging competitiveness in production rather than creating jobs is not helpful. There is now a move to repopulate some of these abandoned villages, both by original inhabitants who had to leave with their families as children and by city folk, seeking, as these often unadvised dreamers do, the "rural idyll". There are programmes on Spanish television about how the new inhabitants are making out in their new lives, living in one or two renovated buildings among the ruins. It is hard and needs an income that does not rely on the land, uncultivated and uncompromising by present day standards. Sometimes whole villages come up for sale, very cheaply, and are bought by foreigners realising (or so they hope) their dreams. How it works out and if any of these forgotten places can be brought back to bustling life remains to be seen.

Circumnavigating the brown torrents of the dashing, jubilant streams, we walked back to our unromantic but practical camp under the jutting roof. There was room for the horses also to be tied undercover with some hay and we went to sleep in our tents to the sound of them eating and shifting in the dark and all the dogs in Hornos warming up for the night. Later I woke to hear the rain had come back, raising a cacophony on our sheltering metal awning and it felt very safe and cosy.

＊

April 22nd
The day we cheated

Marcela took the wheel and Nikki rode with me today. We wore orange reflective jackets as it was dark and drizzly beside the road but shed them when we hit the remoter high country - just in case there were interesting wild animals around. (Olive eating black bears? Gorillas of the groves?) Both horses were stuffed with unaccustomed grass, Luqa was unsure if he wanted his breakfast and Bruma had the lazies all day. I was riding her and, as we trudged reluctantly along at the back, she made unsuccessful lunges at every patch of green, spoilt with treats from yesterday.

We continued to cross the plain which wasn´t a plain at all. Today´s ride turned out to be exciting, even dramatic, and to be honest rather worrying as I began to doubt my pre-planned map on which I had obviously totally ignored the contour lines. First we rode over the railway line, last seen on Day 4 far to the south-east of us on my way to Pedro Martinez. Then we branched off across country on tantalising, open, sandy tracks, climbing into what turned out to be a private "finca", or farm, at least that is what the notices said, though there were no gates.

It was great to be able to stretch the two horses out into fast canters without any risk of shifting a pack on one of them. As we picked our way up increasingly challenging slopes over the mini mountain, we saw just two people in three hours, both on distant hillsides, both working on precipitous olive groves with machinery adapted to the gradient, neither of whom shouted at us or sent us packing off the "private" land. With vistas stretching once again to Ubeda, I began to feel it was mocking me for not venturing all the way there as Penelope did. Wherever we rode in the great bowl of the plain, the little city watched us from the northern rim. Finally we rounded the mountain top and saw the elongated town of Jodar stretched below. The descent seemed long, as so often happens when you are "nearly there", and Bruma became slower and gloomier as we plodded along and the clouds wrapped blackly around us.

Jodar is somewhat scruffy and unattractive on the outskirts and gets better as you penetrate the winding streets of the centre with the plaza at its heart tucked under the well preserved 9th century castle. Penelope, arriving from the north, rode directly into the square where she lodged at the biggest "posada" she had visited on her travels so far, with places to tie one hundred and six animals to the mangers around an enormous cobbled courtyard. (Yes, she counted.) The posada building, though shuttered now, is still there, as is the huge fountain on the other side of the square where La Marquesa drank, dating from 1777 and hardly changed except for some slippery marble steps. Jaysus they do love their marble here, guaranteed broken hips for humans when it is wet and guaranteed broken everything if you happen to have four legs!

Just behind the water trough is the Café Bar Central where

Penelope treated herself to "tortas fritas", crunchy, thin batter with sugar on it, and coffee for breakfast. At the end of the square there is a renaissance church, that, needless to say, she attended, describing an unusual procession to mass: the priest, in black and gold, followed by a man holding a black and gold umbrella which, she points out, is a Buddhist symbol of royalty. They walked down to the altar where they:

"…intoned an extraordinary duet with the "choir" – that is to say one lady in the gallery who played a runny theme on the harmonium and sang "cante hondo" through her nose at the top of her voice. The effect was mesmeric and I could hardly believe my ears."

The Café Bar Central has yellow ochre walls picked out in crimson around the windows, a fine wooden door and brick surrounded windows on the upper floors, the highest with fanlights. Inside it is a bit battered now, but remnants of tiles and a polished counter give an authentic feel if you ignore the widescreen TV showing one of those endless quiz shows..

"From what film did the song ´As Time Goes By¨ come?"
"Grease"…..

In Andalusia stop in any bar for a jar and the inevitable TV will be broadcasting either quizzes or buxom Señoritas singing "Copla" - loud. No, I can´t explain "Copla", you have to come and experience it for yourself.

I met ldelfonso, in charge of all things historical in Jodar. He told me he has another version of "Two Middle Aged Ladies in Andalusia" at home, with more pictures than mine. Oh why didn't he bring it? I would have been ecstatic to see a few different photos for a change from the ones I knew by heart having handed her book round and round in so many villages by this time. Apparently Penelope presented the book he has to a professor from Jodar, Juan Lopez Morillas, and signed it for him. She definitely returned to visit Andalusia after her ride ended - sorting out deaf Fernando's hearing aid in Moclin was one of her projects, though she may have only gone to Granada province. This professor lectured in Granada University. It is possible she stayed on these visits with her friend Gerry, the Duke of Wellington, or his manager, Eudo Tonsen-Rye and family.

The walls of the Casa de Cultura in Jodar were covered with photos, some dating from the early 20th century, and a lot of news cuttings showing such important local events as the rehousing in 1961 of grinning grubby cave children into better accommodation. Idelfonso was upset that the only image in my book that Penelope took of his town was of some very basic houses in the poorest district with cave dwellings below them.

"Why take such poverty when we have beautiful buildings here?"

I tried to explain that hers was a documentary of where she went and what she saw, not an advert for tourism in Jodar! Later I walked up to the top of town and found the exact spot where she took that photo. The free-standing houses are spic and span and, where the caves were is a little park planted with flowering trees. No sign of the troglodytes now. Gone the dirt lane, the goats meandering around and the barefoot children.

When Penelope returned to the great "posada" in Jodar, she unexpectedly found the landlady's sister hard at work scrubbing the landing and the steps at seven in the evening. In her experience cleaning was always accomplished before lunch. The landlady herself was heavily pregnant but continued working away cooking for all the guests and doing the ironing with a flat iron filled with charcoal which she blew into as necessary to increase the heat. Penelope describes the one other member of the family present:

"On a sofa against the wall sat a spherical matriarch. She never spoke....From time to time she beckoned to a boy who without a word would go to a sideboard and fetch a syphon of soda water. The matriarch would squirt some of this straight down her throat and up came her wind in a series of loud belches. I got the giggles but everyone took it as a matter of course..."

During the night, Penelope became aware that the young landlady was having her first baby two doors away which would explain the impeccably cleaned house and granny's distraction. In the morning she called in to see the radiant mother and baby girl, Sabelita, and, unable to find any bunches of flowers, searched the market and found grapes and chocolates.

"The spherical soda-water-drinking matriarch was now transformed by grandmotherhood into a laughing joking old girl. Whereas before the happy event she had just sat and stared into space she now bustled about the kitchen and the yard talking at a great rate and asking me to take her with me on the Marquesa."

I had so hoped to be able to meet Sabelita, a fifty-eight year old woman who would somehow represent the passage of time since the two middle-aged ladies passed by and confirm the continuation of the people they lived so closely with. I was very sad to hear she died of cancer a couple of years ago. I wanted to tell her of her beautiful young mother cooking and ironing in the posada kitchen up to the last minute and all the joy her birth brought. How her grandmother flowered overnight with delight at her arrival and Penelope's search for her gift of grapes. All on November 29th 1961.

211

When I realised I would be a day behind schedule because of the recent bad weather, I chose to omit spending the night in Jodar, partly because finding a way to ride from here to my next stop, Belmez de la Moraleda, had become a problem.

Penelope became very lost in the heart of the Sierra de la Cruz which is part of the Sierra Magina and her description of her ride made me determined not to go so wrong myself.

On the recommendation of the parish priest, she set out via the shrine of La Virgin de Los Cuadros, less than a two-hour ride south of Jodar, but she was unable to ride up into the sierra there because a continuous line of laden mules and donkeys were descending that afternoon, leaving no room for her and her mount. She continued along the road east a little way and then, on the directions of a couple of ploughmen, took a path up the mountain again, having been told to keep always to the left. All she had at this point were a few pieces of torn map dissolving in the damp which did her no good at all and the rain poured down on her and the Marquesa, both enveloped in one enormous black oilskin. As the tiny path became more and more dangerous she started to pray.

"I began to get vertigo because the track had narrowed to a goat path and the mountain fell away so steeply to our left...I found myself reciting the Hail Marys while meditating on wheth-er the scrub of the mountainside was strong enough to arrest the Marquesa and me in our fall."

Eventually her little trail stopped at a precipice dead ahead but she remembered "always to the left" and carried on down as best she could, terrified and worried about having to spend the night out under the rain. She had worked out that she would leave the Marquesa´s saddle on her for warmth, make a tent of her oilskin and, remembering that she had brought bread, a lemon, almonds, raisins and some "filthy brandy", decided she would have enough for her supper, when she heard goat bells and knew she was near a farm. From there she found the road into Belmez de la Moraleda.

*

I had already come on a recce here with ˝Long Jon˝ Addis in February. There was no sign on any map of Penelope's path so first we inspected the alternative by road which was horrific, crash-barriered, steep and unforgiving; somewhere I definitely could not look upon as an alternative to a path across the mountains. After scrutinising Google Earth and every other available map, Jon managed to make his way across what was partially Penelope's route but it was not very clear and deteriorated into a very rocky descent which neither of us was convinced the horses could manage. As is always the case, everyone we talked to knew that there was a way which was totally suitable for horses, and, as is also always the case, nobody could tell us exactly how to do it!

There is a postscript to our route finding, as, when Jon and I returned yet again in August, very reluctant to be beaten by the Sierra Magina, we did work out how Penelope had done it, her tortuous path now disguised by a broad forest trail bulldozed into the mountainside as befits what is now the Sierra Magina Natural Park.

*

So, back in Jodar on a damp April afternoon, I was one day behind my planned schedule in rain every bit as hard as that which fell on Penelope in 1961. I decided to cheat and called upon a friend two villages away, Baltasar, who had that magic carpet, a horse trailer, to come and transport us along the horrible road to Belmez de la Moraleda. We loaded up the two astonished (and delighted) horses, climbed in ourselves and it seemed to me, after three weeks travelling by hoofbeat, in the blink of an eye we were being welcomed by Diego, Policia Local and owner of our Casa Rural in Belmez. Diego was a tower of strength during my time in his village, every inch a policeman, concerned, efficient and anxious that everything should be tickety-boo for us and the horses.

We settled the horses in their little plot, and ventured into the centre of the village. I asked around for the "posada" and after we had sorted out that I meant the "posaa", leaving out that pesky consonant that Andalusians see little point in, (so Granada becomes "Granaa) I was shown the building, de-scribed as quite humble and tiny by Penelope.

The landlord, Diego Cees Gomez and his wife Carmen had a two-month-old baby, Anita, when Penelope arrived there on that stormy evening after her scary ride across the mountain. Diego gave me Anita´s phone number and I found myself talking to a charming fifty-eight year old woman who knew all about Penelope.

She was surely only a baby when she came?

"But my father never forgot her. He talked about her all the time, said how cultured and charming she was, intelligent and full of life. Very well bred! My father died in 2013 and my mother in 2015 so they had good long lives but they couldn´t

214

go on living from the posada; we were just too poor, so in 1971 when I was ten we all moved to Alicante. There my father was a school janitor and my mother cooked."

Penelope mentioned that Carmen was a slim blond woman, so unusual here.

"Yes, blond with blue eyes. My younger brother took after her. I am more like my father."

Anita returns from Alicante for the village Feria every year and stays in the old posada which she says she would never sell. She was not there in April but Diego got the key from a neighbour and we were able to see inside the "tiny posada". Through the front door there are now deep steps where Penelope describes how:

"..a cobbled ramp led down and down into cavernous depths and I should not have been a bit surprised to find the Holy Family sitting at the bottom. I tied the Marquesa to a peg and went on my eternal quest for barley"

Now the stable is furnished with a table and chairs, a mirrored dresser, baskets hanging from the whitewashed beams and lit by a strip light, so popular in all the oldest houses, casting a depressing glare over even the cosiest of rooms. A doorway leads out to a small patio where the stream flowing into a stone basin would have provided water for the animals in the shade of a huge grape vine which certainly predates Penelope´s visit. I found the bedroom up the steep staircase, right and right again where she tripped over the step every time. I know it was that room because, sure enough, I tripped headlong into it too! The same wooden hooks on the walls, and still a rickety, old-fashioned washstand. She was enchanted to find the swiftly flowing stream under a wooden cover in the kitchen floor beneath the "posada" from where the household got all their water. This was how most of the village houses helped themselves to, truly, "running" water. She remarked that it was a splendid solution to the curse of frozen pipes. One feels she may have dealt with that problem rather too frequently in country England.

"We closed up the cover to the stream under the kitchen once the water was piped in," Anita told me. "But it is better than air conditioning in the summer, keeps the house so cool."

We chatted on happily for a while, about her children, a boy and a girl, her life in Alicante and mine in Ronda but mostly about her closeness to her father. I am sure it was mutual, according to Penelope:

"He was mad about his little Anita and prattled away to her as he held her in his arms..."

All over the old "posada" there were photos of the family so I could see Carmen and Diego on their wedding day. Diego small and solemn and dressed in a black suit with eyes and hair to match. Carmen, open faced, also in a dark dress, holding a bouquet of lilies. On the other wall was a photo of Anita, marrying her man from Alicante. She has just the same features as her father and I saw how he would have looked if he had allowed himself to smile for the camera. A photo of Penelope's hosts appeared in the magazine of the August Fiestas of Belmez 2019, with mention of her visit to their posada, possibly inspired by my arrival and enquiries in the spring. They are elderly in this picture, Carmen with her arm around her husband, Diego gazing straight at the camera, hands folded on his walking stick.

The Town Hall in Belmez de la Moraleda is a pleasing old building with inner patio and arcaded balconies and here

Diego showed me photos of the dreaded spectre of "progress" that started the year after Penelope left. Black and white pictures of the chaos engendered when they dug deeply under every street to control that wild stream and then the demolishing of the old stone church where Penelope worshipped to be replaced by a rather nasty modern edifice of which everyone in the village is exceedingly proud. I did gather that the old church was practically falling down which I suppose gave them the excuse to replace it.

Penelope arrived just in time to stay an extra day for the festival of the "Señor de la Vida", the Lord of Life. She sent a "wire" from the telegraph office to the Tonsen-Ryes telling them she would arrive a day later. How antediluvian that sounds now, but also how extraordinary that a tiny place like this would have a "telegraph office". This day of celebrations, starting with fireworks, ending with a clay pigeon shoot and filled in the middle with a lot of Holy Masses and processions, is still celebrated every November 30th, though I am not sure how the musical accompaniment in the new church would compare with Penelope's experience. Her description is a grand example of her self-deprecating humour. First the poor priest transferring a picture of Our Lord from church wall to "anda" or mobile throne.

"He then climbed on a chair and with great difficulty got the picture off its hooks....In lifting it down, however, he gave a plaster statue of Our Lady a great biff so that she rocked in her retablo niche but fortunately did not fall... The choir in the west gallery consisted of five village girls caterwauling the Missa de Angelis accompanied by the harmonium playing not quite the same tune. But who am I to criticise church musicians? I, who in my Anglican

217

days was dismissed from my seat at the harmonium in Baulking village church by the musical vicar who wrote to me saying that 'the disaccord between the instrument and the congregation had become so apparent as to be destructive of devotion.' "

While investigating the village for traces of the two middle-aged ladies, we three blow-ins were intrigued by the frequent mentions of "Las Caras de Belmez", the Faces of Belmez. This phenomenon had begun since their visit, and once again, Policeman Diego, our private oracle, was called upon. He led us to a small village house, Calle Real number five, where a slip of paper on the door showed the telephone number of Miguel, son of Maria Gomez, the first to experience the extraordinary happenings within these walls. He duly turned up to show us round, though he was a little distracted at the sight of Nikki and spent a lot of time gazing up at her. Cupid's arrow hit an instant target there.

Walking into the little house was like stepping back in time. Plain wooden chairs, a sofa with lace antimacassars, a fringe of embroidery along the mantelpiece and glass and china on display in the alcoves. A nineteen-sixties square clock ticking loudly and pictures of little boys dressed for their first communion and newly-wedded couples looking as if they were dreading the night ahead, hung on the walls. Here, in 1971, black and white images of faces started appearing in the walls and floor. These faces changed places, disappeared and reappeared, they were both large and small, male and female but they were very persistent. The house has been emptied of family, locked and guarded by professional investigators, and the images continue to pop up. Every now and then a completely new one is there in sharp relief, but if the house is then left undisturbed the image moves to another site.

As Miguel explained it all, there were a multitude of "faces" on the walls and floors around us, some blurred, some clear as day and some coming into focus unexpectedly as you stared at the surfaces all around. There was a mother and child, a bald man who Miguel said sometimes appears in profile and sometimes full face, another much smaller man wearing a coronet, and an incredibly sad woman under the fireplace. The family tried concreting over but the faces reappeared elsewhere. Scientists from Valencia took some of the faces, cutting through the stone to remove them, and studied them for a year. Within a few days of this, the faces that they had removed reappeared in the house and, when they brought them back, admitting they could find absolutely no sign of human intervention in the rock, the faces that had replaced them, disappeared again.

There have been many more investigations over the years, both by bona fide scientists and paranormal experts and no one has come up with an explanation. A lot of 12th century bones were disinterred from under the house but, then again, the date of the commencement of the much more recent Civil War also turns up beside some of the faces of young men; thus there is really no final conclusion to any of it. So there they are, the continuously self-renewing "Caras de Belmez de la Moraleda", as much of a mystery as when they first started appearing. I wonder what Penelope would have thought? She had no trouble believing the Holy Mysteries and the powers of a multitude of saints, but I have a suspicion her Protestant roots might have rebelled at this phenomenon with its whiff of banshees and things that go bump in the night. I, of course, came out of that little house a true believer with every hair on my body standing on end.

After Miguel had posed for several photos beside "La rubia, la guapa, que fuerte que es" ("This blond, this beauty, how strong she is") aka Nikki, we repaired for a very good supper to celebrate our successful crossing of the great plain. Diego had directed us to the best restaurant in town and, half way through, I was told someone outside wanted to speak to me. Sitting in the drizzle beside that little stream that had been allowed to escape briefly from its pipes to decorate the square, I found Sabina and two other village ladies, all wanting to talk about the old days. So there we sat for half an hour chatting and I could tell they looked upon the weather as a benediction, not a curse. Eventually I rejoined my friends, very damp and only delighted with myself, my phone laden with gorgeous old photos of Belmez downloaded from Sabina´s.

Clockwise from top: Camping with Marcela and Nikki, Penelope´s landlords Diego &
Carmen Cees on their wedding day, Policia Diego helping in the rain.

＊

April 23rd
The miracle of the shrine in the storm

Things went downhill this morning as soon as Nikki and Marcela drove off in my Kangoo to have breakfast in the village and continue on to Sotogrande (Marcela) and Gibraltar Airport (Nikki). They took with them the clothes Aude had lent me, damp and dirty now, and my rubber boots which had arrived with them and I now reluctantly relinquished on my pack horse's behalf. I was preparing and loading the horses in pouring rain and, as I made a pig's mickey with the blue tarp covering the pack in the wind, trying to protect my whole life from getting saturated before we left, my seat (saddle) for the rest of the day was soaking up the downpour. Diego, super sleuth re Penelope's visit, provider of house and paddock to my expedition, and now police escort out of town, helped me heave myself onto Luqa wearing every garment I had brought with me layered under my wonderfully waterproof but awkward Spanish cape. Somehow I didn't take off in the wind like Batman or Dracula but it was a close thing. He then got in his squad car and escorted us up the slippery streets, past the bar with sympathetic citizens peering through misted up windows, past the little stream in the square now gone demented, until the road gave way to mud and I was on my path south along the Sierra Magina. Diego stood in front of me, blocking my progress and said "Are you sure?"

I was not a bit sure, in fact I was mortified with doubts but I was not prepared to drop a day behind again. The last I saw of Belmez de la Moraleda was policeman Diego standing by his blue-flashing car with some ghostly horses leaning over the fence beside him watching us leave. I thought I was hallucinating, perhaps I was seeing the spirits of other beasts lost on the mountain in weather like this?

Off we slithered, along an apparently beautiful path with apparently beautiful views that had been recommended to me by the local footpath information and Penelope herself. She describes this ride as of such beauty that she hated the thought of being forced to return to real life in England within a few days. The deep blue cloudless skies made her previous bad weather seem like a dream. It was well for her, I thought grimly, as the sleety rain came in horizontally and the horses turned their heads away like birds trying to tuck under their wings.

After her fright and near disaster between Jodar and Belmez, she took Anita's father, Diego Cees, along to guide her and stayed at the walk all the time so his donkey could keep up. She describes the trails they took, clinging to the mountainside amongst the pines, the picnic of bread and ham and chocolate they shared and Diego's affection for his little white donkey.

"He patted her on the neck and said "Muy Buena la burra" (such a good donkey). I asked if he fed her any barley but he said he could not afford to. She lived on "paja" and occasional grazing on

which she appeared very fit."

On their ride together Penelope took a photo of Diego on his donkey which she sent him from England. His daughter Anita told me how it became his most treasured possession and he used to show it to all and sundry while he bored them about the merits of the wonderful Englishwoman. Then came the disastrous day when he took it to the park to show his cronies and lost it. They searched high and low but it was never seen again. I bet there is a negative, if not a print, in one of those boxes of Penelope's that went to the British Library.

My journey today was very different from theirs. As we climbed, the wind and sleet battered us mercilessly and I got colder and colder until I sort of solidified in the saddle and couldn't move anything. When I started yawning and feeling dopey, alarm bells went off and I knew I had to dismount and walk with the horses. My wet cape stuck me to the saddle for long seconds as I tried to extricate myself and actually reach the ground and then, mindlessly and relentlessly, the three of us just plodded on. The cloud cover was so low we couldn't see the next tree trunk let alone any views, and I just walked and walked and talked and talked to the horses and gods of the mountains, to the forest and the wet rocks and Penelope. I demanded that they take us somewhere, anywhere, we would find shelter from the wind and rain before we all three got hypothermia. My fury kept me going. I was fed up altogether with the vile weather that had been dogging my enterprise for twelve of the twenty-two days I had been on my ride – yes I counted them as I stumbled along. Why bother to cross southern Spain in spring when you'd get better weather in Connemara in November, and that's falling down with mountains and dripping with views too? I was fed up with never having a dry garment to put on in the morning, fed up with slippery reins and miserable horses and fecking MUD!

Head down, fuelled by rage though still very cold, I nearly walked slap into a white wall which, blissfully, cut out the wind in our faces. I tied the horses up in this haven to a climbing plant as best I could with my blue hands and gave them their nosebags full of oats. Then I felt my way around the building until I came to a door. Miraculously it was open. Even more miraculously I found myself in a chapel warmed by the hundreds of candles that had been lit by the faithful for Easter, only a couple of days ago. Shaking uncontrollably, I started peeling off my drenched garments and hanging them to drip on the ends of the pews. This was the Sanctuary of Fuensanta, a few kilometres from my destination, Huelma. I was no longer lost and frozen on the mountain but thawing out in a 17th century sacred place. The story goes that a Moslem queen of Granada became a Christian and her husband was so furious he cut off her hand. Praying to the Virgin of all Miracles she was told to bathe her arm in the holy spring of this Fuensanta and her hand was restored.

The Fuensanta contains a famous "Belen" or crib, in a glass case filled with little cameos of figures going about their daily lives in caves and by rivers, on rocky hillsides and valleys. The centre of it all is the Holy Family and it is much revered and loved by the folk of Huelma. I turned on the tiny light and examined the mixture of old plaster figures, modern plastic additions – not necessarily in the same scale - and papier maché scenery, made by many different pious hands over the centuries. The chick-pea heads of the more home-made and less important characters made me smile.

Gradually I started to feel more human but I was not home and dried (ha ha) yet. The shortest way to Huelma from here was partly along the main road that runs from Jaen to Granada. Quite a tricky plan on a clear day but, with invisible lorries hissing by in the fog, their headlights appearing momentarily as they passed and disappearing again with a roar, it was altogether too risky. There was only so much I could expect of my trusty reflective jacket, and the luminous bands I had brought to put round the horses' hind legs and tails seemed downright laughable at this point. So, what do you do when you are cold and marooned in a chapel in the rain with two tired horses? You phone one of the Three Kings of course. Who knows more about long distance travel and following their star?

Baltasar, to the rescue again, God love him. It was magical, as he drove up in his little jeep the rain started to lessen and once again I clambered on board my recovered horses, using the sacred spring as a mounting block, and followed him along a track that cut out a bit of road. Then he followed me in his car, all warning lights flashing, for about two kilometres of main road, protecting our backs until I could turn off along a path to the village and his olive grove where the horses were staying. As I left the road and he drove on, four huge lorries and a bus tore past us, raging at having been inexplicably held up by the little jeep. I don't think they realised why or even saw the horses, which means we would have been dead meat without the Wise Man.

Luqa and Bruma were relieved of their sodden gear in jig time and I left them grazing in the lee of the hill and was hustled into Baltasar's village dwelling, blissfully warm and welcoming. Insisting on lending me dry clothes and whipping mine away to be washed and dried, Maria José, the very pretty and welcoming lady of the house, had a warm bathroom, fluffy towels and then hot broth ready for me. I was still very shivery even after all that and nearly fell asleep in my soup. Stifling my yawns and continuing on to potatoes in "alioli", tomato salad and pork chops, I started asking my hosts about their life in the fine village of Huelma, hidden beyond the rain-spattered windows of their cosy kitchen.

They were both born here where they met when they were twelve, fifty years ago.

Maria Jose has never left and Baltasar only went away to study in Granada. He qualified as a teacher but, after military service, he joined the local land registry and has been there ever since. He is a nice-looking man in the true sense, with a really friendly open face, just nice! He explained the Spanish system of urban and property registry which he thinks works well. It means that anyone who pays their taxes and is registered as the owner of a house or land is protected against third-party robbery, violence or wilful damage.

"Huelma is a good village to live in. We have never had "Señoritos" (a ruling class), just a capable, strong middle class. Never huge riches or desperate poverty – just all doing pretty well. There was a big furniture factory here which exported all over Spain but that collapsed when the crisis brought house prices crashing down."

It seems that around here every village is like a little kingdom, with individual ways of going on.

"Belmez is very different; did you see Cortijo Alijares when you rode out? Those are the "Señoritos" there and that family and "cortijo" were fundamental to the whole village. I think they have fallen on hard times now though. Neglecting their olive groves in favour of horses."

That would explain those misty figures I had seen through the rain, standing deep in a grassy grove. My heart warmed to the family who favoured horses over olives.

Baltasar and Maria José then filled me in on other local communities, one where many still leave for the French grape harvest as a matter of course and whose system of agriculture is very different from Huelma, another where violence is endemic, always has been.

"The other day an old man was walking his land and was beaten up and left in a sack in the field for dead, they are all weird in that village, and it is only eleven kilometres from Huelma!"

When I first contacted Baltasar, on the recommendation of someone from Huelma Town Hall, he suggested I left my horses up on his farm for the two nights. However, when I discovered it was going to add about six kilometres to my journey, we decided the land just beside his house in the village was a better bet. Now he wanted to show me his "finca" so, as the rain held off after lunch, we all set out in the jeep to climb up the hills on the far side of the village, looking back at what Penelope described as

"...the best preserved, twin towered toy fortress I have ever seen"

This was Huelma castle, built by the Duke of Alburquerque at the beginning of the 17th century, a rocky fortification that blends into the colour of the pinnacle it is built on, as do all such castles and towers in the Serra Magina, so it becomes difficult to tell where crag ends and castle walls begin. The oldest houses in the village lapping at the foot of its rocky perch are whitewashed and stand out as individuals.

Balthasar farms one hundred and thirty-five hectares of olives and almonds with a gorgeous old battered "cortijo" at its heart. There were happy dogs, cats, hens, horses and a sheep called Pig. His nephew keeps his animals here too, a glorious place for them all looking over the village to the mountains beyond. They explained how they try and keep their farming organic, using solar pumps for irrigation and leaving all the ground cover between the trees for wildlife. No insecticides or herbicides. It is obvious, as with all farming everywhere, that those who do not rely entirely on their crops can afford to be more organic. Baltasar and Maria José have another income so they can allow themselves this luxury and the percentage of loss of harvest that inevitably comes with the old ways. We walked around admiring the new house they have built on top of the hill with stables attached where they spend holiday time and have family meals. Here were two horses that Baltasar never has time to ride, the same story applies to all of the very few horse owners I met on my travels. He sees it as a reason to look forward to his retirement - more time for the horses. His almond groves are impressive. The fruiting this year, predictably after a spring of phenomenal blossom, was record-breaking, some of the trees were so laden with almonds that the branches were in danger of snapping off in the wind.

My horses fed, the wind still blowing and the sky a gloomy shade of slate, I decided my outdoor activities could come to an end for the day. My hostel had a bar where I ordered a piping hot bowl of "Sopa de Picadillo", a grand stand-by for cold weather. Broth with an egg and ham chopped in it and sometimes skinny pasta. Followed by chips which are always delicious here as they are cooked in pork fat which adds to the flavour no end. My vegetarian friends wax lyrical about Andalusian chips - I never have the heart to spoil their fun. Then I just snuggled down into my bed, although it was only eight o'clock which is regarded as tea time in Spain, with my trusty hot-water bottle, filled with water boiled on my tiny gas stove. Haven't seen a kettle yet on my journey. Gradually the whole body shudders from the day that was in it subsided and I started to feel warm all over.

*

April 24th

The boy in the middle who grew up

I borrowed an umbrella from the landlady at my hostel for my morning walk up the long sloping streets of Huelma to the modern Ayuntamiento in a square under the castle. Opposite is the posada, with a particularly wide door to accommodate the mules who came here from the kilns, laden with earthenware "cantaros" to sell in Huelma market. Bartolomeo, son of the landlords in 1961, still lives here though his vermillion features indicate he may spend more time in the bar next door. He was waiting for said bar to open so I had a few brief words with him during which he was near to tears (bear in mind he was already rather emotional about the closed bar) discussing the demise of his parents´ posada. He sadly admitted that the stables, once so bustling with "bestias", now only house his firewood and junk. Also on this square is the Bar Ideal, which Penelope described as the Fortnum & Mason of Huelma. I had coffee there and was shown a "then" photo of the café as it was in her time, the mahogany counter stacked with tinned and bottled delicacies, hams hanging from the ceiling and a variety of tapas on display. Now all that has been replaced by shiny white tiles on which are hung myriad bottles and optics and everything else is mirrored, even the pillars reflect your every move. In fact it was quite difficult to take the "now" picture without appearing in it myself. Penelope admits to having an upset tummy by the time she arrived in Huelma but she still tucked into delicious snacks for lunch in the Bar Ideal. Little did she know what lay ahead, for she was then approached

"… by a wiry little man of about sixty"

He bowed charmingly and handed her a bit of paper with her full name and date of birth, "Penelope Valentine Hester Chetwode. Born 14th February 1910". This was Don Juan Jerez Dias, one of a family who owned three farms in the area and had seen her in the priest's house in Belmez and obtained the rest of her details from the Guardia so that she would feel reassured when he invited her to his house. It was next to the posada, a smart two-story dwelling with a beautiful walled garden, which she loved, and a modern bathroom and loo – which was probably just as well because he invited her for a second lunch and she:

"…could not explain that my inside was in a state of volcanic eruption…We had luncheon at a cosy table by the window: very good chicken broth, fried octopus, raw home-cured ham, grapes and pomegranates."

In spite of obviously being stone mad to shove that lot down on a doubtful belly, she then stayed to get to know the rest of the family. There was Don Juan Jerez's wife, Elena, their daughter and son in law, Juan de Dios Guzman Justicia, and three little boys for whom she drew the dragons at which she was becoming increasingly proficient as she crossed Andalusia. When left to entertain children, Penelope would draw them dragons, with St George killing them in a suitably gory manner as a bonus. She was impressed how beautifully these little boys coloured the drawings in with their crayons. She found them an attractive and happy family and, after the necessary devotions in the Renaissance church, went back for tea. This included bread and BUTTER, a huge treat thanks to the Fresian cows on the edge of this village, honey, two plates of red and black salami and coffee. This is proof, if we needed it, that ladies of the British Raj do not let a little thing like "Delhi Belly" get in the way of their social commitments.

The info man at the Ayuntamiento sent me back down the sloping streets to the office of Paco Ruiz Sanchez, the "cronista" (historian) of Huelma. A serious and knowledgeable member of the Town Hall, he let me blather on about my journey for a bit and then produced a translated copy of all of Penelope's pages about Huelma and the nearby villages. So it turned out he knew far more than I did about her stay in this lovely large village, really a town now with six thousand inhabitants. He then showed me a wonderful photo of the three little boys who coloured in the dragons, all mounted up in a row on the Marquesa, by the church under the castle, their father at her head. Both this photo and another of her riding out of the village, Penelope had sent back by post to the Guzman Justicia family, the first colour photos ever to be seen in Huelma.

He started, very unnervingly, to plan the presentation of the book I was going to produce about my trip in Spanish. While I tried to damp down his enthusiasm suggesting he "didn't sell the bearskin before hunting the bear" – Spanish version of "not

233

counting your chickens", the door opened and in walked... a small wiry man in his sixties. He resembled the father of the three boys holding the Marquesa in the photo and was, of course, one of the boys! The one sitting in the middle to be precise, Juan Francisco Guzman Jerez, known as Don Cisco.

"Of course I remember Penelope, we called her Penelope Valentine – easier for us to pronounce. I remember the hat, the broad hat, and oh yes, she had very rosy cheeks, like yours."

That, sir, is called weather-beaten and what, may I ask has happened to Spring in Andalusia? But I didn't say that of course, and anyway he forestalled it with a "piropo" (flirtatious remark) about my eyes. Get away out of that you flatterer you!

"I remember she was a big woman – and a woman above all! Nobody did those things then, least of all a woman. We thought she was very exotic! We were very honoured she came to our house. We had a fine house because our maternal grandmother, Elena, was adopted and brought up by the noble family in the castle and she inherited it. When my brothers and I got married we divided it into three. The garden is still there but now it is an enclosed patio."

Cisco, with his neatly trimmed white beard and an enthusiasm that was contagious, was a fund of information. He collects antique arms and "Barros Malagueños", the 19th century figurines of "bandoleros" and "viajeros romanticos" (travellers, poets and painters) made by Malagueñan artisan, Jose Cubero. These used to be sold throughout Andalusia by pedlars. Now they are very valuable, and mostly kept safely in museums. He had brought a couple with him, faces of real people, every knot in their colourful ponchos detailed, a pipe in the hand, a "bota" of tooled leather. He can't WAIT, he told me, to have more time to investigate and learn about the history of everything and everyone, particularly armaments. Oh yes, and his favourite hobby is surfing the net for antiques.

"You were in Illora? I am fascinated by Native American history, you know. There is a Sequoia there planted from seed by one of the Duke of Wellington's forbears and the tree is named after an Indian Chief. I love the origin of words, don't you? The river in the valley below us is called the Jandulilla, taken from the Moorish word for Gracias a Dios. That is what they say to each other when they belch, you know. And that is exactly the sound the little river makes going through the rocks. Names are important. I have two daughters, one called after her great grandmother, Elena and the other after an Italian opera singer I really liked, Mari Micaela, and we added Fuensanta as well for our Sanctuario."

He imparted information to me at such speed I could hardly keep up with my notes and it was Don Cisco who solved the mystery I have been wondering about all my Spanish-speaking life. Why on earth is the nickname for every José I have ever known "Pepe"? To explain this I need to tell non-Spanish speakers that the letter "P" is pronounced "pay" in Spanish.

"Well" Don Cisco grinned mischievously. "José (Joseph) was the father of Jesus, right? But he wasn't, was he? God or the Holy Spirit or one of those fellas had got there first so José was only the "Pater Putativo" (supposed father) or PP! Therefore "Pepe".

Are his brothers as chatty and full of information as he is?

"One of them is worse than me. You can ask him anything and if he doesn't know it he makes it up!"

I'd say the whole family could be a branch of the well-known O'Guzman clan from Blarney.

At lunchtime I discovered that Luqa had lost a front shoe. I was not surprised as the kilometres we were doing (around three hundred so far) were wearing the toes of the iron horseshoes through, and I expected his to go before Bruma's. She picks her dainty little clogs up and puts them down again with plenty of flirty knee lifts. He does the cool dude shoe shuffle, sloping along with a minimum of extra movement, sliding his feet across roads and rocks. One of his front shoes had just fallen apart into two halves and the other was well on the way there. Baltasar, who seemed to have a solution to everything, was already in touch with a farrier who was coming all the way from Granada. Our host in Huelma was indeed the sort of lovely man who would look after you in any situation. He could, as they say, "mind mice at a crossroads".

Blas the farrier turned up and did an efficient and fast job, helped by shoes ready made to fit Luqa that I had lugged in the pack all the way from the start of our trail. While he hammered away he was, of course, curious about my ride and, when I mentioned Gaucin, it turned out he had served his apprenticeship with my regular farrier, Sergio. As they say in Spanish "The world is a pocket handkerchief." He charged me a ridiculously small amount for the shoeing and nothing at all for his long drive to get to us and when I objected he said it was the only way he could be part of my adventure.

The rain let up a little after lunch and Baltasar and I set out leading my two rather tousled and muddy mounts to a high road under the castle with views across the village roofs to the church. Here Penelope took a black and white study of a muleteer leading his animals along on a warm sunny day. My plan was to reproduce this picture as best I could with Baltasar as Penelope the photographer and me as the muleteer. The similarities were obvious, the view of the castle and the church and the old village houses had not changed, and, although there were more houses, unlike other villages, they seemed to blend into the whole without shouting "Look at us, we are modern and don't fit in!" The expression on the horses as I led them up the hill about five times to get the right shot was certainly just as resigned as the mules'. There was a new tree that interfered with the vital spot and a very obvious electricity cable crossing the view, and, where the 1960's muleteer had been in shirtsleeves in the sunshine, this one was in a thick jacket, scarf and woolly hat! Eventually, after pausing to let the occasional truck by – another new development – we managed a fairly satisfactory replica of that long ago day and led our "bestias" on down to the church. It is a grand old building and the photo of the three little boys was taken beside it. However, due to a previous Mayor's overenthusiastic reform of the church plaza, it is now a ski slope of marble and we couldn't take the horses to the exact position. We had summoned Don Cisco to participate in this re-enactment. One of his brothers lives out on the farm and was in the middle of some vital olive preening or pruning and the other was travelling, so he turned up alone and held my two horses, the background of the houses on the street unchanged and crowned by the "toy fortress", while I took the photo. On the way back he presented me with a flower, definitely pinched from someone's window box.

"Green eyes, orange flower, Irish flag. There was a wonderful singer called Fatima Mulcahy, did you ever hear of her? I'll see if I can get you some more information."

Now I am absolutely sure he made that up…

From top: Bar Ideal as it was in Penelope's time. Bar Ideal Now. Don Cisco, in PC's photo, the little boy in the middle on Marquesa held by his father and in the same place 58 years later with Luqa, Mimicking PC's photo f the muleteer

238

April 25th

Visiting the casino and circumnavigating the bog

My next stop, Montejicar, is only fourteen kilometres from Huelma so I planned on leaving after lunch today when, unbelievably, the forecast said that the rain would stop.

Penelope took the little road all the way and then carried on another twenty kilometres to stay in Campotejar, but I decided to make a shorter day of it, mainly because the position of the second village, right beside a flyover carrying the Jaen to Granada motorway, put me off. Studying the map there were some nice tracks and paths between Huelma and Montejicar which would enable me to avoid the road almost completely but, luckily, when I mentioned this to Baltasar and family, alarm bells went off with them because the "campo" in this area is known as particularly sinky when saturated. Sure enough, a few phone calls and emails later, it turned out I had mapped my route through a veritable quagmire where Luqa and I would surely get deeply stuck and portly little Bruma possibly disappear without trace. So I resigned myself to clattering along the narrow road.

This morning I had an appointment with Juan Luis Guzman, grandson of the owner of the Bar Ideal in Penelope's time and part time guide. Juan Luis also works for the Town Hall in communications and we had coffee, in said bar of course, with the Communist Mayor, Francisco Ruiz Garcia. He was somewhat edgy as local elections were imminent and the TV was on full blast with the latest predictions and discussions just above our heads, so he mentally absented himself from our conversation, listening with one ear to the furious arguments going on between the political parties. Also with us was Chema Garcia, town councillor for education who runs a language school in the old prison building where he teaches French and English. He and Juan Luis kept up a barrage of questions and information in Francisco's stead. All three men were young, funny and attractive, far from the image of stuffy old "Town Hall-ers" and indeed Huelma has the most active social media sites of anywhere I went on my travels with almost daily posts on Instagram, Twitter and Facebook about plots, plans and parties in the village.

Juan Luis took me upstairs in the Bar Ideal to the "Casino". In Andalusia the word casino has little to do with gambling and everything to do with a private club, often men only. Penelope felt very honoured to have a drink here "…as if I had been asked into White's" (an exclusive gentlemens' club in London). She and Elena, Cisco's grandmother, were the only two women present accompanied by the doctor and the mayor. The mayor spoke very good English and she taught him the expression "Raining Cats and Dogs". I thought how appropriate as I looked out of the upstairs window of the now empty casino which is only used for functions, at the umbrellas

bobbing along in the plaza below. In fact Mayor Don Prisco
Benavente has a street named after him in Huelma. He used his
linguistic skills in French and English to give the very first language lessons to the children of the village in his free time with
the help of vinyl records. Although Penelope does not mention
the doctor's name, it seems it may have been Doctor Paulino,
a much loved local physician who practiced in Huelma all his
life and, now in his nineties, lives in Granada. I was invited
back to the Ayuntamiento where the mayor presented me with
a jumbo tin of olive oil (what else?) and various pictures were
taken. I accepted graciously, silently apologising to Bruma.
As pretty well everyone in Huelma had read the translation
of their section in Two Middle-Aged Ladies, they seemed to
know what I was about and it was really great not having to
endlessly explain my "raison d'etre".

Then Juan Luis and Chema took me on a tour of the
very beautiful 15th century church which Penelope had tossed
aside as *"Over restored inside with no interesting works of art"*,
hurting the feelings of pretty well everyone in Huelma who
read the translation! It is more of a little cathedral really, built
with the apricot-coloured stone of the area. Standing on the
site of another more ancient church, building work started
on this newer place of worship in the mid 1500's. It is known
as one of the most notable examples of 16th century religious
architecture in the Province of Jaen and, once again, the archi-
tect Andres de Vandelvira was part of the team that raised it.
The outside is really magnificent, though somewhat marred
by being marooned in a sea of unsuitable white marble. Inside
it was standing room only for holy figures and saints. Some
with their garments forming part of the carving or mould and

some wearing real clothes. This custom of dressing holy statues is very popular, with favourites like the Virgin of Guadalupe having a variety of different garments. Our village saint in Gaucin, the "Santo Niño" (Holy Child) lives in a chapel up by the castle except when he ventures out for his Romeria in August, and in the vestry is a glass fronted wardrobe with his outfits. A huge colour range, heavy shiny fabrics with brocaded decoration, there must be thirty different little gowns for our little saint. Stitched and created with love by generations of devout local ladies, the array of rich vestments make one feel that at any moment Henry Vlll´s pages may come in and get ready for a state occasion.

Unfortunately this dressing the icons up in real clothes has meant that the woodcarvers´ art is under used and only the oldest statues show the wonderful talent of these artisans. Every saint has his or her "day" of course, as well as coming out en masse over Easter, and I realised even my two modern companions, Juan Luis and Chema, were encouraging me to admire "their Virgin", "their Christ figure" "their saints", such is the loyalty of everyone involved to the "Hermandades" (or brotherhoods) of "costeleros" who carry the holy ones out on special occasions. Baltasar and Maria José´s son, rather to their bewilderment, actually goes many miles to carry saints out of other churches in other villages while in the queue to be one of the chosen ones here. I am a Catholic, I come from a country where miraculous Virgins are reported to weep in country lanes (and I mean the plaster variety – the flesh and blood virgins are few and far between and their condition does not last long, mainly because they don´t waste time weeping in country lanes) but all this passion, power and rivalry involving robust young men stalking round the streets with graven images on their shoulders is a mystery to me.

The statues that I remember in the Church of the Immaculate Conception in Huelma were Simon of Cyrene, hands held out to help carry the cross. He would be put on the "anda" behind Christ and his cross, helping share the load at Easter. There was a very sweet-faced Virgin too who I think was an old sculpture, she didn´t have the moist glass eyed dolly stare of those ladies dressed in black and representing anguish, sorrows, pain and the like. One niche held a nice little figure of Jesus, in shades of pink, riding his Palm Sunday donkey and my favourite was an angel with huge golden wings ploughing behind a pair of oxen. A suitably bucolic holiness for a little town in a valley of rich brown soil under the misty mountains.

At three in the afternoon the wind was still blowing but the showers were further apart so, against my protestations that there was no need for all of us to be frozen, with the help and company of Baltasar ("I do it for love of the horses") and Maria José ("But are you warm enough? Why not postpone until tomorrow?") I once again loaded the pack on Bruma, balancing up the weight in a new way to take into account the addition of my gift of olive oil, heaved my saddle and sheepskin and saddlebags onto Luqa, mounted up and rode out from the village of Huelma that had made me so welcome.

As we jogged along the quiet road to Montejicar that climbs and turns, drops and straightens through the rolling countryside, I felt very sad that my journey was nearly over. Beyond the stretching pastures to the east, just over the brow of the curving arable fields was Eloy´s cortijo, nestling by Domingo Perez, where I spent my second night on the road sitting before that blazing olive wood fire. Further on towards the horizon was the vertical hill with our lost nose bag, our Everest, that we had scrambled up to reach Pedro Martinez where the snow caught us unawares beneath the blanketed-white Sierra Nevada.

Penelope, on a clear day, took this very road I was following and, as she crested a rise, was treated to the panorama of the chain of glistening white mountains to the south. Today they were crouching behind the scudding grey cumulous and I could not get even a glimpse of them. However, looking back, the horses and I could see the majestic Sierra Magina along whose pine-clad skirts we had trudged two days ago. Then, we saw nothing of the massive rocky gorges and outcrops we had passed above in the thick mist but now it all looked quite impressive.

Suddenly the letters on the kilometre markers changed from JA to GR and we were back in Granada – or "Granaa" - province. I made up a song about our adventure and sang it at the top of my voice to the empty hills, the deserted road and to my two friends, Luqa and Bruma, who had carried me over mountain passes and along hot, dry, endless trails, through bitter winds and snow, deep mud and tiny perpendicular paths. They listened to my song without noticeable reaction for quite a while and then Luqa stopped dead and had a pee, which could have been a comment.

Montejicar sits in a bowl surrounded by little rounded summits. From the top of one of them a chapel looks down and from another a camouflaged fortress, indistinguishable from the rocks it stands on, surveys the village. Manolo, known as "El Ingles" (The Englishman - he isn´t), my contact and helper here who had found a billet for my horses in Fernando´s barn, had told me everyone would be in "el campo" this afternoon. There was something important happening in the world of Montejicar farming, some vital bit of land husbandry which meant the whole village emptied and, do you know, I never did find out exactly what it was. Worn out with sentiment and singing (me) and eager for another overnight stop with supper in the offing (Bruma and Luqa) we clattered through deserted streets. There were silos, tractor sheds, mechanics shops and agricultural paraphernalia everywhere showing that this was somewhere that took its agrarian responsibilities seriously. I turned the horses out beside Fernando´s barn where they completely ignored the beautiful hay that Marcela and I had delivered a week ago, nearly losing the car in the mud, and fell upon every sort of unidentified greenery that had grown up overnight in the moist air. They looked well, fat and shiny, considering the distances we had covered and I felt proud that I had managed to keep them like that. How their heads were, I wasn´t too sure. I would have liked to ride on for ever and never stop but they had started asking me some questions in their gait and manner as we rode out of each old place and into each new. It was too subtle to put into words but I sensed they might be getting a bit thin and tired in their minds, if not in their bodies.

There was a bit of a hiccup getting into my hostel as the owner had had to go off to hospital with a family member (the only able-bodied person not in the campo – or maybe she was really) but left me a message that mother-in-law would bring me the key. I waited so long in the empty square I was sure there was a muddle but when poor Ma-in-law turned up I couldn´t believe she was the person they had chosen for such a mission! Obviously the only citizen of Montejicar left in town – "Dear, dear, not even able to drive a tractor in the campo" - she could hardly walk at all, just a teeny-   weety shuffle and the last ten metres took her long minutes. She made up for her physical challenges by greeting me effusively and deafeningly and turning the key in the lock to a very comfortable hostel indeed.

Kind Juan Luis from Huelma had forwarded the photos taken this morning with the mayor, in the "casino" and the church. Glory be! I looked like the wrath of God with sodden "hat hair" and a brick red face. Penelope is remembered for her high colour; obviously the searing winds of the Sierra Magina destroyed her complexion too!

*

April 26th

A foxcub, a skinflint and a pig's elbow

Montejicar, silent and empty when I arrived yesterday, came to life at seven in the morning today, many of its two thousand inhabitants making their way to the "campo" once again with tractors, trucks, 4x4s and diggers. This little hard working town is as bustling as Huelma but in a more agricultural style. I found Luqa and Bruma blissed out in the first sunshine they had seen for ten days, balancing on the stilts of drying mud wedged in their hoofs, eyes half shut, soaking up the warmth. It was just as well they did not need any shelter as Fernando's barn, which he seemed to think I could clear out myself and use, contained the usual collection of detritus, built up over time. There were drainage pipes, metal rods, pallets, a television, cartons, boxes, rolls of wire, a broken wheelbarrow and a lot of corrugated iron sheets, just waiting to slice through an unsuspecting tendon.

Generally not easily moved.

On the way to see the horses I passed groups of men clustered outside the mechanics´ shop as their tractors were fixed or oiled or re-fitted . There was a digger with a new shovel being screwed on and an automatic olive tree shaker adjusted. The onlookers were chatting as they hung around waiting, much as their forbears would have waited while their mule was shod at the blacksmith´s forge or the saddler replaced worn leather on a harness.

*

On one of the early recces I did back in January, I had driven through these olive groves beneath the Sierra Magina for several hours during the olive harvest where slow-moving tractors sailed around like elephants in their native land, holding me up endlessly on the narrow lanes. The favoured signs seemed to be temporary triangular exclamation marks, plonked at intervals along the verges, usually before perpendicular hairpin bends, making me wonder what on earth could be on the other side. It was usually just more tractors, more nets, more men and, above all, more olives. For a time I had been sure there must be goats somewhere as I saw their little blackcurrant droppings at intervals scattered all over the road. After many kilometres of never seeing an animal, it dawned on me that these were undersized, rejected olives left over from the harvesting. Sadly I was to learn that goats or any other livestock were highly unlikely around the busy olive-growing centres like Montejicar.

Penelope had ridden through Montejicar, only stopping to ask a Guardia Civil the way to Campotejar, so she missed a really good church! From the balcony of my "Hostal Rural" there was a splendid view of the church tower above the tiled roofs of the village. It had a Roman numeral clock face, illuminated at night, that struck the hour and the half hour until midnight when it tactfully stopped chiming until seven in the morning. This tall stone tower was built in the mid-16th century, shortly after the mosque that was already there was converted into a church. Inside it is partly grand and gold-leafed, although the wooden ceilings give a feeling of antiquity, and when I explored deeper into the interior under the tower I found a fascinating font. It is carved in softest pink marble which I think is called jasper rose with black lion heads in another stone at its base. All very smoothed by centuries of holy water and loving hands, it took me ages to get a good enough photo of the crest on it to go online and find out what it was. However, having for once good wifi reception and a lazy morning, I investigated and discovered it was the crest of Juan Mendez Salvatierra, Bishop of Granada from 1577 to 1588.

The continuing story of this ride has the magical soundtrack of birdsong. Rain after four dry months had brought out the best in the infinitely-varied feathered choruses along the way. Being very ignorant of the individual songs, I had tried to identify some, but the people I talked to often only knew a local nickname for the bird which was not even the Spanish name so it was not as easy as I had hoped. Firstly, of course, and without rest or pause, day and night, to the extent that I think they must sing on shifts, the nightingales. Wherever there was a drain or a stream, a puddle or a spring, and that was everywhere this moist month of April, they were trilling their descending scales, followed by series of clear whistles from their tiny throats. Then there were turtle doves

crooning to themselves in the taller trees and the hoopoes'
echoey bell like tooting, and electric blue thrushes lifting their
little hearts from the tippity tops of the olives. I recognised the
goldfinch, almost always visible as he sang, which is more than
can be said for most of them. Then there were various warblers
and the multiple trilling of the vividly dressed bee-eaters. At
night the owls serenaded us in rather gloomy competition with
the unquenchable nightingales. I went to the local library in
Montejicar to try and find out more, but they didn't have any
good publication on Andalusian birds at all. While I could
have read all about Amazonian parakeets, there was no book
to help me identify the local songsters. The girl in charge, dark
haired and pretty, made notes of my suggestions though, and
agreed with me they need more information if they are to have
tourists like me. I don't think anyone had ever asked for local
information about the "campo" before, it is just something you
know about because you have lived here all your life. She was
also rather excited about my journey and told me how much
she missed her grandparents and their mules and horses tied
up at the drinking places in the village. (Not sure if she meant
the inns or the water fountains...)

My friend and contact in Montejicar was Manolo "El
Ingles". Even he didn't know how he obtained this nickname
but he has always been known as "The Englishman" in his village and the bar he owns is called "Bar El Ingles". He is a kindly
man, probably in his sixties with a certain aura of a life perhaps
lived a little too well. Now semi-retired, his daughter served me
in the bar and he and his son run a "venue" for functions which
seems to be working well. I was put in touch with him because
he used to have a horse and therefore had accommodation for

said horse in the barn he subsequently sold to little old wobbly fella Fernando. So it was he who had originally introduced me to Fernando who had agreed to let my horses stay there the two nights. Manolo kindly offered to show me a good way to proceed tomorrow as I was still a trifle nervous of the treacherous earth which could become so boggy after all the rain, but I did not really want to stick to the road for another day's riding. We set out in his truck and it soon became obvious that he was a man after my own heart, a country sportsman, so we spotted partridge bursting out of the bushes, rabbits cruising the arable fields and fox spoor along our way. There really were masses of rabbits, they must be a total plague to the farmers here. In my part of Spain there are none at all but I think the welcoming crumbly soil in this part of Granada province makes for better burrow-building than our solid rock outcrops. I could sense my companion's itchy trigger finger, longing for the season to open so he could eliminate some of these pests.

Manolo told me about a fox cub he rescued and is bringing up with a litter of pups at home. He found it out in the fields a few weeks ago, completely alone with no trace of the vixen. He showed me a video of the cub with its adoptive family and it looked as if the pups were on the racist side and the little fox was having to fight its corner. However, the bitch was letting it suckle along with her family but he reckons soon she will start to complain about its teeth which grow sharper sooner than the pups, and at that point he will put the little wild animal on dogfood. Manolo has other hunting dogs which he is sure will kill it once he lets it loose among them so, as we drove along the winding lanes, he was on the phone to his nephew to see if he would like to take it. Even though he strokes and plays with it every day to domesticate it, Manolo told me there will always be a risk to poultry with a tame fox. You have to keep them well away from your chucks or they simply can´t resist the instinct for an honest-to-God massacre. After our afternoon exploring I felt I had tomorrow´s route entirely sorted out, avoiding long stretches of the hard road, thanks to "El Ingles".

I called in to see Fernando at his house and pay him for my horses´ stay and the "grumpy old man with a heart of gold" turned out to be a "grumpy old man with a heart of greed"! After I had placed in his outstretched hand the amount I pay everyone for the horses´ overnight stays, in this case two horses for two nights, he continued to hold out his open palm, digging me in the arm for more. I was really taken aback, especially as, although I always offer to pay, a great many people along the way have not let me, even supplying free hay. In the case of Fernando´s barn all we in fact had was a small stretch of rough land around it and water from the hose. The hay, the oats, the buckets and everything else necessary I brought with me. I pointed this out to him and he said I could have used the inside of the barn if I had wanted to - after I had spent a week clearing it out I suppose - and if he had known he would get so little money he would never have let me take the horses into the enclosure! Anyway, I ended up paying him way above the norm just to get rid of him, and still it wasn´t as much as he wanted. I think if he could, he would have kicked the horses out on the street there and then. It was the first piece of non-generosity I had come across and left a nasty taste in my mouth. Bad cess to him the old begrudger.

I had pig´s elbow for supper in the bar by my hostel which was extremely tasty. I decided to follow the trend and take a picture of it as it arrived sizzling in its earthenware dish. When I looked at the photo later it looked absolutely disgusting – but it wasn´t!

*

April 27th

The beauty of the ride and the dreaded overlap

E arly on a blue-skied morning I walked down to the barn and balanced the pack saddle for the last time on Bruma's little round figure. Somewhat hastily, because I really didn't want to have to set eyes on greedy old Fernando, I led the horses through the gate of their enclosure, closed the padlock and left them tied in the street while I raced quietly up some steps to put the key back in his mailbox. He might well be a fitful sleeper, waking in the night worrying does he owe himself money?

Then I hopped aboard, so easy without all the rain gear, and clattered through the village. From Bar El Ingles we were waved off by all the early morning customers, sipping their café coñac and anis chasers, obviously essential as a precursor to a day on the tractor in your olive groves. "El Ingles" himself saw us onto the trail he had shown me yesterday, rising gently out of Campotejar.

We dawdled along, stopping at any excuse for a graze, standing at troughs for ages contemplating the possibility of another drink, taking pictures of a sunlit landscape. The truth was I didn't want to arrive today. This was my last day of setting out alone with my ride horse and my pack pony into the unknown. At lunchtime we would start to overlap with our second day out and, lovely as that route was, I would know what it looked like, felt like, smelt like, I would remember what was round the next corner. So we dragged our feet along the little paths, over friendly low hills, arable-planted in the dips as olives cannot cope with frost pockets. There was oat straw, ready to harvest, and two kinds of barley, one with jolly red whiskers. As we climbed a little higher, among olives and almonds, the great white godfather of all the mountains ranges we had known on our adventure appeared to the south, glistening against a cobalt sky. Buenos Dias Sierra Nevada! The peaks would now watch over us to our journey's end.

The time has come to give up my secret....Luqa is not mine - any more. He used to be half mine for about eight years, and he worked hard carrying the good, the bad and the ugly (and a lot of very nice riding clients too!) over the hills and far away for seven months of every year. Then I would hand him back to his other fifty per cent owner, Corky Addis, in the next village down the hill where he was her main equine, much loved and galloped round the cork forest! When I retired and sold my business and I reckoned I could not afford to keep more than two horses for myself, I sold my half of our dear Shaluqa, the Moorish name for the wind that sweeps across Cadiz, to Corky. Shortly afterwards, I decided to go on this adventure across the provinces of Granada and Jaen. Rather belatedly I realised my second horse, Romero, another dun, would have a nervous breakdown if I asked him to move on every night for thirty days. He goes off his food for forty-eight hours if he changes fields.

Corky, when I mentioned my quandary, immediately offered me Luqa, without any hesitation or conditions of any sort. A real friend is gold; and so today the three of us were riding to meet up with her. We would spend the night together in Colomera and then she would ride the last day of this venture on her own lovely Luqa.

I am so glad I brought two horses. They have been such good friends throughout, reassuring each other in threatening situations, minding each other in all the unlikely places they ended up for "Bed & Breakfast". Often staying a fifteen or twenty minute walk away, I would have been anxious leaving a horse alone overnight, but knowing there were two of them, I could relax and let them get on with being horses. Although I always have a working friendship with my equines, and we have great fun together, I never lose sight of the fact that they are HORSES, and I can therefore never replace the company of another horse for them. The herd mind set is so embedded in their species that they are never happier or more relaxed than just hanging out with other equines - horses or mules or donkeys. This fact is often overlooked by owners who try to "humanise" their horse or keep them permanently in a stable, thus depriving them of social interaction. I remember in Ireland we had an ex- racehorse who came to our farm complete with his cuddly toy, a sheep. The big thoroughbred and the baaing woolly thing were inseparable which we thought was sweet but it has to be admitted the other horses viewed the whole thing with distaste – the new arrival was definitely kinky!

My two companions on "La Ruta de Penelope" were very different in character, Bruma, brought up in Ronda in the rough and tumble of a yard full of mules, being quicker on the draw when it came to getting under fences, undoing door catches and generally looking after herself and her round shiny tummy. I frequently found Luqa watching dumbfounded from inside the enclosure where they were supposed to be - obviously - enclosed, while Mademoiselle grazed and explored outside.

"How did she do that?" he seemed to be saying.

Bruma also tethered well, tangled ropes held no mysteries for her, a skip and a jump and she'd sorted it out. She would mind herself under any circumstances and absolutely nothing worried her. Luqa, on the other hand, put one leg over the rope and then froze. I really think he'd have waited all night for me to come and deal with it rather than risk another move. In the end I would tether Bruma on a long line to graze at lunchtime and just leave Luqa loose, knowing that he would never stray far from his best mate.

Luqa's talents were different. He was our water diviner. Maybe a gene inherited from all those desert-crossing Arab ancestors. On warm days when they hadn't drunk for a while he would stop dead beside a field or grove and sure enough there would be a water trough over on the far side, or a tiny stream hidden in a nearby ditch. Sometimes it was very disappointing because the trough was in an empty farmyard behind a locked gate, or the water he could smell was coming out of a pipe filled with little holes to irrigate the olives and not accessible to us. But in the high sierra he came up trumps several times, finding forgotten mossy, green, drinking places where long ago beasts

of burden had quenched their thirst for hundreds of years before us.

After about two weeks on the road, he developed another
quirk. As long as it was after lunch he would choose places
he thought it might be really nice for us to spend the night.
Screeching to a halt at the entrances to farms and "cortijos" he
fancied and gazing longingly over the gate with heavy hints
and sighs, he was often quite difficult to move on. He was
choosey though, they must have a nice vibe and other animals,
if only a dog. He was particularly insistent about farms with
goats which were few and far between. I spent five minutes
today trying to get him to move on from one little old farm lane
where there was a herd of skittish black and brown goats. I
think they reminded him of his home – which he had obviously given up all hope of ever seeing again! There wasn't a scrap
to eat where we halted so Bruma, impatient as usual, finally
put a stop to his stubbornness with a sharp nip on his shoulder.
Apart from the companionship between them, having two
horses gave me the option of swapping their jobs around, and,
although I was very lucky and they didn't get any serious rubs
or saddle sores, if they had, I could just exchange the gear on
them as the riding saddle and pack saddle make contact with
their backs and bellies in very different places.

We found a wonderful glade of knee-deep grass beneath a
once-stately, ruined "cortijo", with palest pink walls, grey and
white where the bones of the building were showing through,
matching the rocks all around it. Poppies filled every crevice of
the tumbled stones where it was gradually collapsing into the
meadow and a cuckoo, very close at hand, saluted us insistently
throughout. As usual I hadn't thought very hard about my lun-

cheon (as Penelope would have called it) and munched on some bread and a very squishy banana (inevitable saddle bag damage means bananas don't survive very well) but I think that was the best midday snack the horses had all month. So I sat in the shade with them and wrote my journal while they crunched and tore at the lush green and never lifted their heads. I read the second last chapter of Penelope's journey, while I was experiencing my own second last day along the trail she initiated nearly sixty years ago.

"The track led over undulating farmland with the great mountains bounding the southern horizon. I do not think I have ever seen a more beautiful landscape, even in Kashmir. I rode along physically feeling the silence, my senses quickened by the knowledge that the tour was ending and my partnership with the stolid old Marquesa must be broken, perhaps forever."

In fact I don't think it was because, according to Manolo in Moclin, she rode back several times over the years from the Duke of Wellington's estate in Illora to visit her friends in the hilltop village, and I would say there was a strong possibility she was once again mounted on the Marquesa. Penelope carries on to say many complementary things about the people she had met along the way, things that may have surprised her more than me because, living in Andalusia, the warmth of their welcome is an everyday experience. She finishes:

"The innkeepers and their wives and children, my fellow guests at the "posadas", the families who put me up in their houses, the parish priests and their curates, even the much-abused members of the Guardia Civil, had all been out to help me. I had enjoyed the most friendly and unselfish traits in their characters which, added to the extraordinary beauty of their countryside, made me feel I had

259

ridden through the garden of Paradise before the Fall."

Snap! Also, to this list from the "Middle Aged Lady", I would particularly like to add every single person who emerged from a town hall or "Ayuntamiento" to direct, explain and introduce me to others in their village. Everyone had time for me on my little quest, everyone was interested, helpful and "simpatico".

It was no good foostering beneath our magic "cortijo" any longer, we had to continue. As we emerged onto a lane, Luqa did one of his sudden halts and we saw a long stone water trough across the fields and picked our way round the edge of the crops to get to it. Sure enough is was filling to the brim from a clear spring, running from the rock at one end and overflowing into a concrete culvert at the other. I filled my water bottles as the horses drank deeply. A young man, loading firewood into a truck, walked over to us.

"They only re-channelled that into the trough this spring. We want to encourage "Turismo Rural" and there has to be fresh water available for the walkers and the cyclists. They may put a sign up to it from the lane. It is really good to see it used."

Oh, how I would love to help with the dream of rural tourism in this magnificent part of Andalusia. Perhaps "La Ruta de Penelope" walking trail can become a reality.

Shortly after our drink we came to a T-junction and turned right and both horses changed gear, lifted their heads and lengthened their strides. At last, something familiar! We had come to our overlap. Along here we had ridden out, still in some trepidation and anxiety, towards our night in Domingo Perez. However this time we were heading the other way and my reluctance dissipated as I felt the equine engines beneath

260

me increase the revs and looked at the straight road before us through two pairs of pricked ears.

We reached a petrol station on the outskirts of Campotejar, with the busy motorway flyover roaring above us. Gone, for the moment, the solitary road, the silent fields. The horses tied happily under some trees in the car park and were much admired by two French families on their way home after the Easter break. Luqa politely accepted some bread from them and Bruma, not so politely, ate a ham sandwich out of the hands of one of the kids. Luckily they all thought it was hilarious. I went and got something unhealthy from the shop to supplement my banana, took off the pack saddle so I had something to sit on and we waited for Corky. The young guy we had seen at the trough drove past in his truck and spotted us, raising the roof with hoots and waves so then everyone was looking our way as if we were celebrities!

After a four and a half hour drive from the Serrania de Ronda, Corky turned up with her horse trailer and she and Luqa were reunited. I was pleased she thought the horses looked really well. I thought so too but it is always nice to have confirmation.

Penelope, who did not have the luxury of friends turning up with horse transport at this point, had spent the night in Campotejar and then ridden directly to Illora but I had decided to cadge a lift to Colomera, thus skipping about three hours of overlapping route which would have added up to a forty kilometre ride today which seemed excessive. We would ride to Illora tomorrow, via Moclin because we had a lunch invitation there, and I also wanted to see Manolo, historian and sculptor again.

It was something of a small homecoming to arrive back at José Eduardo´s stables in Colomera and to his family´s warm welcome at their little hotel "The Posada de Colomera". It was also fun to have Corky to share the evening and my (probably rather tedious) chat about the past weeks of riding and exploring, taking my mind off the sinking feeling I was experiencing as emails and WhatsApp's started bombarding me now everyone knew my journey´s end was imminent.

Back in the posada where it all started, where I came on my very first, very tentative recce last November, I slept like the dead.

✳

April 28th

Colomera back to Illora

Brilliant blue skies and a hot sun making a jeer of me after all the days of cold and wet, Corky now riding her Luqa, the pack stowed in the car and only a few essentials in our saddle bags. I hopped up onto Mademoiselle Bruma and we rode out from Colomera. On this, the last day of our odyssey, we were once again flanked by José Eduardo and some of his riding clients who had never been on a horse before. I was already familiar with his relaxed way of taking complete beginners riding but Corky was fascinated. Horse prepared, they clambered up from whatever side they chose, he put the reins in their hand, whichever hand they preferred, and then moved their hand with his. "Right, left, stop." Then grasping their leg he indicated how to work the accelerator and we were off, the beginners in the lead.

Of course the secret is in the temperament of the Spanish horses. In spite of being portrayed as fancy flouncy yokes with an excess of flying mane and tail, underneath the Andalusian horses are supremely sensible and can turn the ballet on and off as required.

Having spent a large part of my life working with them, I can honestly say that for sheer common sense in the equine world they are unbeatable. A young horse may shy at some "bogeyman" beside the track the first time he passes but next time, and for the rest of his life, he will ignore it. As it didn't attack him before why should it now? Traffic, barking dogs, sheets flying in the wind, worry them far less than their foreign riders who are used to other races of horses and fear the worst. You can see the thoughts going through the Andalusian's head "Why is she all tense and patting me? What's the matter with her? Did I miss something? Is there something hiding behind that very noisy lorry?"

Relax, look at the view, have a chat and your good-looking mount (and they are all sweet on the eye) will take you safely along tiny bohreens and rocky ridges, beside busy main roads and across wooden bridges. Anytime you ask they will come up with a bit of showing off at the "Romeria" or dressage in the arena. Tie them up outside the pub on a bustling village street, haul your toddler up in front on your huge prancing stallion to ride to the Feria, have a beer in the saddle beside the dodgem cars, just don't worry. The Spanish are the most relaxed of riders and this definitely adds to the sensible behaviour of the horse, an unstressed rider has no nerves to transmit to their mount.

Having said that, Lusitanos from Portugal are definitely more spicy and if you pop a drop of Arab in an Andalusian horse the common sense factor can be a diluted, though, apart from anxiety about big lorries, this does not apply to the lovely Luqa!

So more power to José Eduardo who gives his clients their first experience of riding as a sunny saunter in the olive groves for an hour or so, spectacular views in all directions with the Sierra Nevada sparkling on the horizon, lots of chat and laughter and no one taking it all too seriously, least of all José. Of course they return to ride with him.

After just over an hour they turned back and Corky and I continued cutting upwards to a high path skirting the mountains to the north. We were searching for the same view that appears in one of Penelope's photos. She is posed on La Marquesa with Moclin and its castled crag above her head. It took us a while to find the spot as there was a lot more vegetation on that particular slope now. I took full advantage of having someone with me who could take some photos of us today and we started with Corky taking a couple of Bruma and me in what we hoped was the right place. Bruma did her best to pose in a La Marquesa like stance but she lacks the larger mare's elegance. I think we both looked a bit less intrepid adventurers and somewhat more Pony Club than the original photo taken in 1961.

We continued along the shoulder of the hill down to the village of Olivares and its perpendicular and shiny streets. Leading the horses down was a lot less work than walking up, as I had done not so long ago, and I had the benefit of knowing just where the drinking trough was so they could quench their thirst as the morning heated up. It was in Olivares that Penelope branched off to head straight back across the fields to Illora and Molino del Rey but we had promises to keep in Moclin so we started the long climb up the Camino del Gollizno where I had met the disappointed Frenchman on my way down. I got off again on the sheer concreted part, but this time going uphill, as Bruma did not have the new shoes and studs that Luqa had and was slipping quite badly. She walked in front and paused for me, red-faced and banjaxed following in her wake, turning her head and neck back to peer down at me with an old fashioned leer. "Now, who was calling me fatty?"

Our arrival, panting, into Moclin was unexpectedly chaotic. Today was the Spanish General Elections and this is always an excuse for a jamboree of some sort. The village was heaving with mountain bikers racing, runners running, and cars parked far and wide. There were bars set up in every direction on the green space below the castle where I had planned on tying the horses. What with the starting hooters for myriad races sounding off every few minutes, the officials organising through loud hailers, the bars churning out hip hop, rap and "cante hondo" (look it up!), I don´t know how anyone had time to vote – or if they even intended to. We hitched the horses to some shrubs at the far side of everything so they too could enjoy the music and the loud hailers and probably visits from curious children, and walked away. (See previous paragraph about Spanish horses!)

I had been given an introduction to Ian Rutter and Andrew Watson by a mutual friend, Manni Coe, whose company Toma & Coe run some of the very best boutique tours in Andalusia. If they were friends of his I was definitely going to get in touch and I did, as soon as I came to Moclin for the first time. Now, on my way home, I was taking them up on an offer they had made when I rode through a month ago,

"Come to lunch on your way back."

At the time the remote possibility that I would make it all the way and actually be coming back, as I boasted, a month later seemed pretty unlikely to me, though I tend to ooze confidence when confounded so everyone thinks I never have a doubt in my head. Yet, here we were, safely on the final strait of my PLAN eating Ian´s homemade empanada with Corky to add to the mix. Their house, which I first saw as a heap of tumbled walls and potential in bleak November on my recce with Marcela, had turned into an almost-finished welcoming and gracious space, gazing gloriously across the "vega" to the Sierra Nevada and Granada. No wonder the Catholic King and Queen spent six long years in the castle of Moclin aching to reclaim that magical city from the Moors.

Our hosts run Granada Concierge, a company that organises creative holiday courses right here in Granada in such subjects as Spanish cookery, painting and flamenco. Andrew is also a graphic designer, specialising in children´s picture books, and Ian a radio broadcaster so I seemed to be in the right place for someone who was flinging random sentences like "When I write the book…" around.

Full of food and good company, we reclaimed our mounts from the noise and the frolicking up the hill and rode away down the lane towards Puerto Lope. Such a long climb it had seemed when I was coming up, late for my date at the Ayuntamiento of Moclin on two not quite fit enough horses. Along here we found my friend, Manuel the historian´s, "cortijo", La Fragua, (the forge) nicknamed La Miseria because he says his grandfather was such an old skinflint, always moaning about imminent ruin. However La Fragua suits it much better because it is here that Manuel makes, casts, manipulates and designs his works of art in various metals. When you walk into the courtyard in front of the "cortijo" with tall trees, an old garden, and views to the "atalaya" crowned hills, the sheer variety of his pieces is unexpected and just brilliant. His ideas are broad-ranging and original and come from so many different sources. Literature, poetry, cinema and theatre are some of his loves, Antonio Machado and Garcia Lorca his muses, so here are impressionistic portraits of Hitchcock and Chaplin, Don Quijote, Romeo and Juliet and many more. He has taken a disc of metal, twisted a vague stooped form and given it a walking stick and – there he is - "Experience", or "The Lovers" or "Friendship". "The Model" is just ribs on legs and "Liberty" is four pieces of wrought iron tube and a flat solid disc which lifts your heart with her freedom leap. I loved his series of smaller Picasso-esque bullfighting models. The matador´s poise, the bull´s leap, the cape centre stage, every move in the sacred ritual depicted and, as for the spectators, there she is, the lady with the "mantilla" sitting high on her head, the peasant with his cap diminished by the conceited Señorito in a sombrero – all suggested with a minimum of the material Manuel uses to sculpt.

Corky and I wandered round with big grins on our faces as we explored this prolific artist´s work. She fell in love with "Liberty" and bought it for Jon´s birthday present to be picked up in the car so it could leap for freedom in their garden and Manuel gave me a little racehorse tearing along with a lean, round-shouldered jockey on board. One piece of narrow wrought iron casually twisted to depict it exactly.

By the time we left La Fragua the horses were riding jealous through the hot afternoon, the scent of imminent arrival hastening them to keep a nose in front of their companion if they could. We passed Pepe, a goatherd, who had wished me well on my first day out. He was watering his shiny goats at a rushing steam which had been barely an excuse for a trickle a month ago.

"Back from the 'Romeria' then?" he asked with wry understatement.

Passing alongside busy Illora, we crossed squares of waste ground, made glorious by hundreds of poppies and, once again, posed among them for photos of each other, our faces rosied by the scarlet reflection bouncing up, everything seen through poppy-coloured spectacles. A little further through the olive groves and there was the gateway, left open by Ramon, to take us once again into the green and pleasant acres of the Duke of Wellington. No mist by the lake this time, but the crops had ripened and acres of peas, grown to feed the partridge, stretched away on either side of the pathways, the elegant aqueduct standing out above it all. Once again the horses and I, and Corky for the first time, rode the long back drive to the main house where those comfy straw-filled stables were waiting.

Penelope remarked that ;

"Returning a borrowed horse to a southern Irishman and an Andalusian groom was a pretty tall order as a more horsey combination could hardly be met with. But conscious of the Marquesa's rippling muscles and glossy coat I was full of self-confidence as I rode her into the yard, which was justified by Eudo's complimentary remarks and the groom's ear to ear grin."

Don Javier, Ramon and Emilia perhaps did not quite appreciate how good my two companions looked after more than three hundred kilometres but they gave us a tremendous welcome and I had a real feeling of a job well done. We waited in the gathering dusk as the sierra turned pinkish mauve to the south and the April night settled upon us. Eventually, José Eduardo turned up to fetch us in Corky´s car, unhitched from the trailer for this purpose as, in spite of having driven large trucks much of his working life, he does not now possess a car. We unloaded the two equine heros' very well earned supper and gave it to them side by side behind their green stable doors. I felt very emotional to think this moment, the feeling of the three of us relaxing after a long day of adventure with another unknown trail tomorrow, would not happen again. It would probably never more be my honour and delight to be the herd leader to the combination of the gorgeous nut-brown gentleman with his kindness and endearing quirks and the bumptious little blond, with her flirtatious looks and capacity for hard work. Eat up lads, tomorrow you only have to walk up the ramp of the trailer and down again.

The drive back to Colomera seemed a long way. It was all a bit of an anti-climax for me but I was so lucky to have good friends like José Eduardo who had come all the way to pick us up this evening after a long day riding with three lots of clients and then seeing to his twelve or so horses. Not forgetting Corky´s help. More than four hours towing an empty trailer to come and get us and another four hours home again with the two horses on board tomorrow. Doing me the most enormous favour.

Having supper in the one and only bar open in Colomera, I spotted the long loping stride of three dark-skinned immigrants flitting along the shadowy street, probably sub-Saharan. I had seen small pockets of them in my wanderings through the villages of Granada and Jaen, always a little apart from the Spanish, safe now but not belonging. Their journey, who knew how harrowing, had ended in a strange place where it would take them years to belong. Mine would end in my own home place with the welcome of a whole village. There is a Spanish expression for those of us who are born lucky.

"Tiene una flor en el culo"

Yup, I am one of those lucky people. I have a flower up my arse!

Clockwise from top: Bruma waits as I stagger up Gollizno. Final farewell to Don Javier and Ramon. Poppies! Talking to the goatherd.

＊

April 29th

Our storiy's end

Such was my relaxed state this morning, when we set out from Colomera to pick up the horses for the long drive home, that I completely forgot about hitching on the trailer. We were bowling merrily along in Corky's car, chatting away, and well past Olivares when I glanced in the wing mirror and realised we were about to arrive at Molino del Rey and load Luqa and Bruma into the...back seat? So we turned around, somewhat shamefaced and rather relieved not to be spotted by José Eduardo who had bade us farewell ages ago.

All the organising, remembering and responsibility had suddenly been taken off my shoulders and I was scarcely thinking at all.

Having got the rig stuck in the inner sanctum of the stables on our arrival with Dan, I suggested we loaded the horses outside the stable yard near the chapel, now the archives, where Penelope asked God to bless her intentions before she set out on November 5th 1961. He was definitely on my side too. Here I was safe and sound, mission accomplished.

Thank You.

Horses on board and ramp closed, Corky turned the car and trailer easily around the circular flowerbed and drew away, while I waved like mad out of the window at our little party of Molino del Rey supporters and friends.

I watched the olive groves and the rolling hills, the not very picturesque little hamlets and the battered "aldeas" drop behind as we left Granada province for Malaga. I remembered the sense of bleak nothingness which had been my first impression when I came here six months ago. Then, I could not understand why Penelope had chosen this empty landscape for her ride and felt rudderless at the thought of setting out towards the deserted skyline in her hoof prints. But now I knew better. I knew the lilac and lupins along the banks of the bohreens and the scudding dragon clouds above the plain of Ubeda. I had experienced the softness of the pink grey hills in the gorge north of Guadix and watched yellow butterflies sipping from a turquoise stream called the Guadalquivir. I had met a man who made carriages by hand in an almost horseless world and a dog who attended mass and a shepherd smoking a cigar. Now I knew the bars with their generous tapas, the "Ayuntamientos" with their generous help and the people with their generous hearts. I knew how the children and grandchildren of these small places came back year after year to celebrate the "Romerias" and "Ferias" with their people. To be enfolded within the whitewashed walls of a place where their antecedents may have suffered hardship and poverty but which, thanks to loyalty, hard work and the ubiquitous olive, still exist to welcome them "home". I knew that every settlement, however small, humble or scruffy, knows how to party, how to have fun, how to laugh and feast and clap and dance.

So, if I had learnt all this about her route, what had I learnt about Penelope Hester Valentine Chetwode Betjeman, my guide for the last twenty-eight days?

From following her trails and paths I knew that she was valiant and revelled in the countryside and its ways, much as I do. The discovery of hidden valleys, of streams and lonely hillsides ran parallel to the discovery of the villages and their inhabitants for both of us. Her knowledge of history, architecture and art put me to shame and made me realise how much time I had wasted gazing out of schoolroom windows dreaming of adventure and exploration. Penelope was also staunch and kind, living and listening with the humblest of people, far removed from her own way of life, understanding and liking them, as they liked her. Her wry sense of humour struck a chord in me many times as I journeyed through the Andalusian mentality as much as the countryside, but she was never condescending or patronising and, for someone born in 1910, and brought up in rather a grand family, she fitted in without any problem, mainly because she was genuinely interested. Occasionally she makes a remark in her book which is considered horrifically politically incorrect now, such as thinking that the children were maybe better off running free in the villages than with too much education, but that is just a woman of her time speaking her opinion; (And anyway, as I had seen, when good schooling finally became available the kids all got educated beyond their village and left, leaving empty houses and halving some of the populations – swings and roundabouts...).

Her distaste at seeing the new ways taking over from the old, such as those tractors she spotted near Pedro Martinez, is very typical of her class and nationality. To this day I hear British people bemoaning the rash of new bungalows in the West of Ireland replacing the old thatched "cabins". Fair enough so, you go and live in a damp bothy with no one left to replace the rotting thatch, filled with turf smoke, cold in winter and colder in summer and see if you don't long for picture windows and central heating!

I think, like me, Penelope would abhor the endless landscape of olives until she understood, as I now do, the modicum of prosperity they have brought to this land so the villages can still survive and the people live comfortably - with cars and televisions and tractors. However, to what extent can I say I know someone just because I did what she did for a fraction of a year of her life and read what she said about it?

Unloading Bruma in Gaucin while Luqa carried on with Corky to Jimena de la Frontera, twenty-three kilometres further south, caused some serious equine bewailing. In fact both spent the next twenty-four hours neighing for their boon companion which considering there was good grass and other horses in both places, speaks a lot for their friendship through thick and thin. For Bruma to waste grazing time was unheard of.

I walked home from her field as my car was still with Marcela in Sotogrande. In dazzling sunshine with cloud shadows, the mountains of my adopted home, the Serrania de Ronda, put on a show. Crowded round the ridge our village hangs on, they tumbled below and above, up close and personal, more intrusive, more flamboyant than the rocky reaches of Cazorla or the solemn distances of the Magina.

OK, my mountains, you are pretty glorious and it is good

to be home, after all.

Maybe in a week or two Corky and I could take the two friends for a ride right here, out to lunch at a bar I know, no protein shakes allowed.

Penelope Valentine Hester Chetwode
1910 - 1986

"Everyone has his weaknesses: some people run after women, others after Dukes; I run after priests and along tracks which, with their alluringly sinuous ways, are gravely tempting me to throw all my family duties to the wind and to go on riding along them forever"

– Two Middle-Aged Ladies in Andalusia

Acknowledgements

Firstly, my thanks for help and advice from John Murray Press, the original publishers of '*Two Middle-Aged Ladies in Andalusia*' in 1963, where Penelope's photos first appeared. Also my gratitude to Eland Publishing Ltd. who brought the book back to life in 2012 and kindly gave me permission to use quotes from it.

A huge thank you to all those who helped me with preparations, advice and equipment, starting from when I announced that I had this "PLAN". Pedro Godino Martin, Mayor of Gaucin, who gave me letters of introduction to every Town Hall along my route. Jose Eduardo Escudero Camarero of the Posada de Colomera who knew the horse trails locally and showed me the wonders of Wikiloc. Jason Howe gave me my wonderful tiny stove and invaluable tips from his personal experience. The Addis family – Jon for advance exploration, the younger generation for struggling to bring me into the world of iphones, and Corky for the loan of Luqa, transporting us home and sterling work proof reading my manuscript, after which I was forced to discover where the hyphen was on my Spanish keyboard. Kelly Destrake for my splendid pack saddle and Rusty Willeford for showing me how to use it, describing the world it would open up to me. Sue and Alberto Saro, for willingness to take on my menagerie at home while I absented myself for a month. Elisa Mirangels who tramped the Cazorla mountains with me searching for overnight stops for the horses, Dan Willeford who drove us to the start of our adventure and Tito Gomez who saved the day with the loan of his truck. Support and advice from CuChullaine O'Reilly of The Long Riders'Guild.

On the trail I found help and interest from so many people I hardly know where to begin.

Illora. The Duke of Wellington who very kindly invited my horses to stay at Molino del Rey and his manager Javier Henriquez de Luna, plus Ramon Gamiz Morales and his wife Emilia who all made us so welcome.

Moclin. Manuel Caba Forja, local historian, who showed me round and Ian Rutter and Andrew Watson in Casa Higueras who were there with encouragement on the first day of my adventure and a jolly good lunch on the last day. Andrew designed this book and I am so grateful for his help, and talent.

Domingo Perez. Mayor Eloy Vera Utrilla, and his father Eloy, for lending us their Cortijo and telling me so much about the village.

Pedro Martinez. Mayor Juan Antonio Fernandez for safe stables in a snowstorm, and recounting all the shared memories with Jose Antonio Lopez Mesa.

Villanueva de las Torres. Mayor Pepe Vallejo Navarro for his interest in my project and introducing me to the relevant people. Juan Valle Martinez and Doña Encarna Rodriguez Gil for vivid recollections of the old days. Paco Rubio Esteban and his wife Julia, for making my horses so welcome in Lucero's stable and showing me the cave houses.

Hinojares. Jose Coronado Iscamez, sister Pili and family, for luxury accommodation, both equine and human, and so much information about local history, and trails in the Sierra de Cazorla. Maria Tiscar for telling me about her life as a child in the posada in Pozo Alcon.

Tiscar. Angel and Juana, Nazaret, Rocio and Cristina Bautista Fernandez for their wonderful welcome when I could find nowhere for us to stay in Don Pedro. The horses appreciated the girls' adoration and I was privileged to talk to granny Maximiliana before her memories flew away to heaven with her.

Puente de Las Herrerias, Cazorla. Cristobal Flores Naranjo for letting us share his little oasis.

Cazorla. The Town Hall for giving us the key to the bull-ring, Hotel Puerto de Cazorla for looking after me so well and historian Don Juan Antonio Bueno Cuadros for his time and help.

Quesada. Juan Antonio Lopez, Cultural representative, for his stories of friends Zabaleta and Navarrete. Antonio Navarrete junior for permission to use his father's poem "Reflexion en Otoño". The Town Hall of Quesada and the

Zabaleta Museum for permission to reproduce the painting "Girl with Still Life"

Hornos de Peal. Victor, friend of Jose Coronado. Though I never met him, his sheltering "roof" was invaluable

Jodar. Idelfonso Alcala Moreno, historian, for a fascinating meeting.

Belmez de la Moraleda. Diego Martinez Sanchez, host and guide with a wealth of information and photos. Sabina for chat, enthusiasm and photos of how it used to be. Anita Cees for memories of her parents and the posada.

Huelma. Baltasar Serrano Garcia and his gorgeous wife Maria Jose, who saved me from the storm on two occasions, warmed me up, fed me and even found a farrier for Luqa. Mayor Francisco Ruiz Garcia for his welcome and gift of olive oil, Juan Luis Guzman Jerez for guided tour and Francisco Ruiz Sanchez for great historical information and introducing me to Don Cisco.

Montejicar. Manolo "El Ingles" who gave me every kind of help in this village.

Finally, my faithful delivery teams who drove many hours to bring me horse feed, extra vet supplies, dry clothes, encouragement and whiskey. Diana Paget and Sally Von Meister, Ian and Aude Baillie, Marcela Stirling and Nikki Bartlett.